CW01646636

Glasgow on a Plate

Chris

December 24

The third book in the series of
Glasgow on a Plate

Thank you for a fabulous
night in No 3

Lorraine x

Food by Glasgow's finest chefs and restaurants.
Edited by **Ferrier Richardson**

Introduction

The first edition of Glasgow on a Plate was twenty-five years ago. So, with this updated edition I can once again showcase my wonderful home city of Glasgow.

Having travelled the world in various professional roles for the last twenty years, it is interesting to see how the culinary landscape has changed within Glasgow.

The most dramatic change I've noticed is the growth in the high-end, casual dining scene and this is the area I have chosen to cover most extensively in the book. No longer do diners, wish to pay homage to a plate or be cocooned in an environment they feel uncomfortable in, they now desire high-quality cooking in a relaxed environment, with knowledgeable, friendly service to complement it.

Even though the book has an emphasis on high-end fine dining, there are a wide range of restaurants highlighted from 'traditional' Italian restaurants such as La Lanterna to the newer fine dining venues such as The Gannet which have revolutionised Glasgow's dining scene. Not forgetting the innovative dishes being served up daily at Ox And Finch or the irresistible fusion of the finest Scottish produce with the best of Indian spices and flavours on the menu at Swadish, one of Glasgow's newest award winning Indian restaurants.

Three things stand out from the testimonies of the head chefs and restaurateurs in this book. One is the sheer commitment and dedication they have to their craft and serving their customers the finest quality available. The second is their passionate advocacy that Scotland has some of the finest produce – game meats, seafood and vegetables – in the world on our doorstep and their commitment to working with local artisan suppliers to maximise sustainability and seasonality.

Finally, and not least, after one of the most challenging periods brought on by Covid and lockdown, their sheer perseverance and commitment to bounce back and continue with thriving venues. These people are survivors. Glasgow on a Plate 2024 provides not only a great selection of recipes from some of Glasgow's finest chefs, but also provides, in their own words, a fascinating insight into their back story, their 'food philosophy' and some of the challenging episodes on their journey. And also, how they manage day-today, making the most of their staff and cooking first-class food for regular local Glaswegians as well as visitors from across the world to this incredible multi-cultural and cosmopolitan city.

Having returned to my home city and opened a successful, award-winning gastro pub in Glasgow's east end, The East End Fox, with a loyal customer base and fantastic support, I am aware of how vital a "core loyal" customer base is to a restaurant's survival especially in the challenging times we have just come through.

So, I encourage you, not only to try these great recipes within your own kitchen, but get out and support all these wonderful venues, bring your "On A Plate" book with you, ask the chef to autograph their chapter, let them know you have had a great experience, remember to praise your server and when you get home, please give them a great review on social media such as the The Glasgow Good Food Groups Social page to encourage others to visit.

Thank you for supporting the book, but more importantly thank you for supporting all the restaurants within the book and the wider Glasgow hospitality community, without your support we could not exist, and all our lives would be poorer for it.

Many thanks,

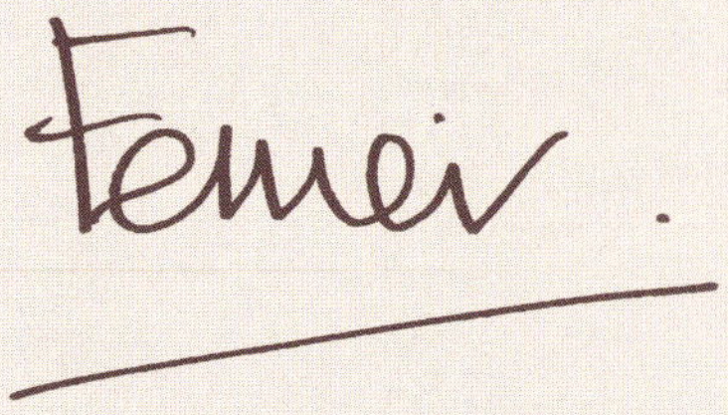

Ferrier Richardson

Canon

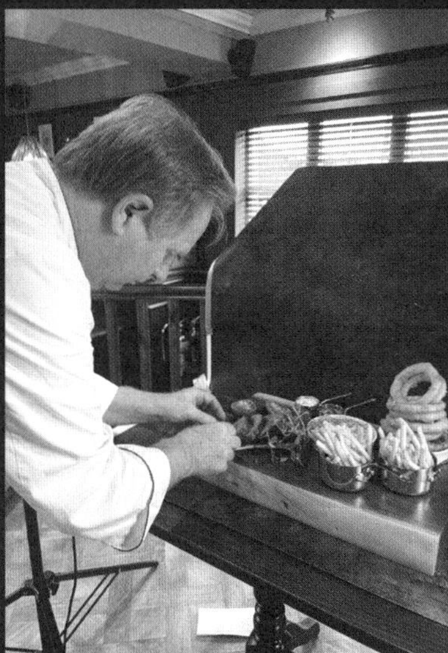
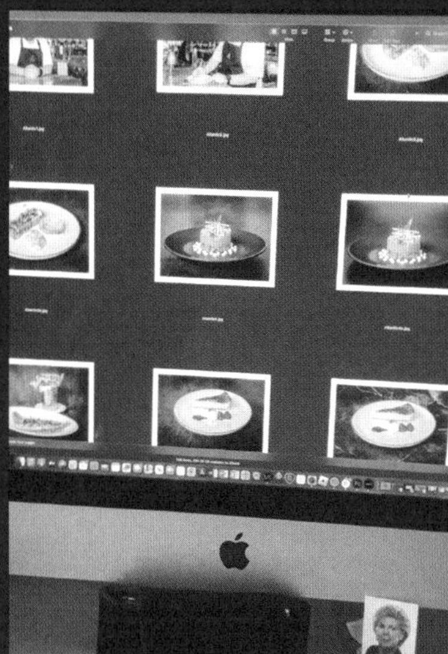

PRIVATE
DINING

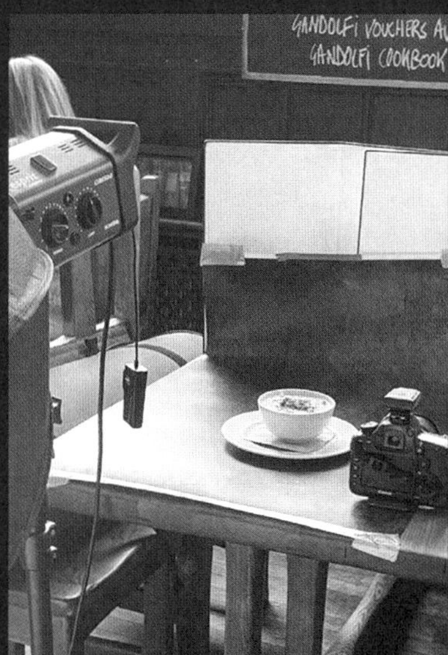
GANDOLFI VOUCHERS AV
GANDOLFI COOKBOOK

First published in 2024

FR On A Plate

Glasgow, Scotland

ISBN 978-1-3999-9828-4

Photography

Amanda Hemphill

Design

River Runs Deep

Copywriting

Alex Meikle

Administration

Vicki Robertson

Editor

Ferrier Richardson

Print

J Thomson Colour Printers. Glasgow

All rights reserved. No part of this publication may be reproduced, stored in a retrieval system, or transmitted in any form by any means, electronic, electrostatic, magnetic tape, mechanical, photocopying, recording, or otherwise, without the prior permission in writing of the publisher.

All recipes in this edition of Glasgow on a Plate have been provided by the chefs and restaurants featured. We are not responsible for outcomes of any recipe you try from the book. You may not achieve the results desired due to variations in ingredients, cooking temperatures, typos, errors, omissions, or individual cooking ability. You should always use your best judgment when cooking with raw ingredients such as eggs, chicken or fish and seek expert advice before beginning if you are unsure.

WORLD LAND TRUST™

www.carbonbalancedprint.com
CBP2296

Foreword

It's hard to believe that it's been almost 35 years since I first stepped into the kitchens of Restaurant October, under the guidance of Ferrier Richardson. For me, that was the beginning of a journey that would not only define my career but shape the chef and the person that I am today. Ferrier didn't just teach me how to cook; he shaped my understanding of what it means to be a chef, and his influence has resonated throughout my entire career. His impact on Glasgow's food scene is immeasurable, and it's something I carry with me every time I step into a kitchen.

Back in 1999, when the first Glasgow on a Plate was published, I was incredibly fortunate to be part of that project. It captured a moment in time when Glasgow's food scene was just beginning to blossom, and the book became a testament to the vibrancy, creativity, and character of this city's dining culture. To be invited once again to contribute to this new edition feels like coming full circle. It's a celebration of the amazing talent that has emerged from Glasgow over the years.

This new edition of Glasgow on a Plate takes the legacy of that original book and elevates it, reflecting how much the city's food scene has grown. It continues to showcase the very best of what this city has to offer, from dining rooms that have stood the test of time to bold and innovative restaurants that are crafting some of the best food in the country. Glasgow's chefs have continued to push boundaries, drawing from tradition while embracing modern techniques and global influences. The result is a culinary landscape that is as diverse and dynamic as the city itself.

This book is more than just a collection of recipes and restaurant profiles – it's a fitting tribute to a city that has given me so much, and to a mentor who helped shape not only my career but also Glasgow's evolving food culture. Whether you're a chef, a food enthusiast, or simply someone who loves this city, I know this edition will inspire you just as much as the original did.

Gary Maclean
Masterchef: The Professionals – winner.
Scotland's National Chef.

Acknowledgements

Glasgow on a Plate 3 is long overdue due to the changing face of its culinary scene and the quality of the excellent chefs operating in the city today.

In order to showcase these wonderful restaurants and their chefs you need an exceptional team of a great writer, designer, photographer and administrator.

I believe one of my strengths is that I can put together award winning teams, be that for an international culinary Olympic team, a charity event to raise money for a great cause, a high-class restaurant, a five-star hotel opening or for a Head of State.

On this project, if I can be so modest, I feel I have exceeded myself. Glasgow on a Plate 3 would not have been possible without the creative flair and organisational expertise of the following.

Stuart Gilmour, from River Runs Deep who has designed the book from top to toe and has way exceeded my expectations, for anyone who has any design projects in the pipeline, Stuart is truly exceptional and anyone who knows me will know I do not dish out praise without it genuinely being earned. Thanks must also go to Marie his lovely wife, who has not only been responsible for printing the book but introducing Stuart to me, thank you Marie for the introduction, your man is amazing as are you.

Amanda Hemphill, for her wonderful photography and her dedication to the project. It has been a joy working with you on this project Amanda, your enthusiasm and dedication has been a constant throughout the project, and I look forward to working with you on further On A Plate books.

The amazing and wonderful Alex Meikle who has brought the chef's words to life and dance on the first page of each chapter, it has been a joy Alex, your dry humour kept us all going throughout the project and as Tina says, you are simply the best, I can't say anymore.

Vicki Robertson, who has been responsible for bringing it all together, an arduous task for anyone, given the difficulty of getting hold of chefs, getting them to respond to deadlines, recipes, need I say any more. To be fair I did highlight this at the beginning of the project Vicki, so I make no apologies! Thank you for your tenacity and professionalism throughout this journey, the book would not have been possible without you.

The talented Gary Maclean for his introduction to the book. Gary and I go back to the late eighties when he worked in my first restaurant October in Bearsden as a young chef. I hope I played a small part in his wonderful career to date, as he continues to champion the hospitality industry in his role as Scotland's National Chef. I am so proud of you Gary for all you have accomplished and more importantly the way you conduct yourself and represent the nation on a worldwide basis. I am forever grateful that you have made time to make this wonderful contribution to the book.

To all the wonderful chefs who have contributed to the book, without your culinary talents this project would not have been the same and I hope you all feel the project team have done your talents justice, showcasing your beautiful dishes.

Lastly to you the reader, without your support this book would not exist and for that I and everyone involved with the project are forever grateful. I hope that each chapter will encourage and inspire you to visit and support all the restaurants within the book.

Many thanks,

Ferrier

Ferrier Richardson

DUCKCLUB

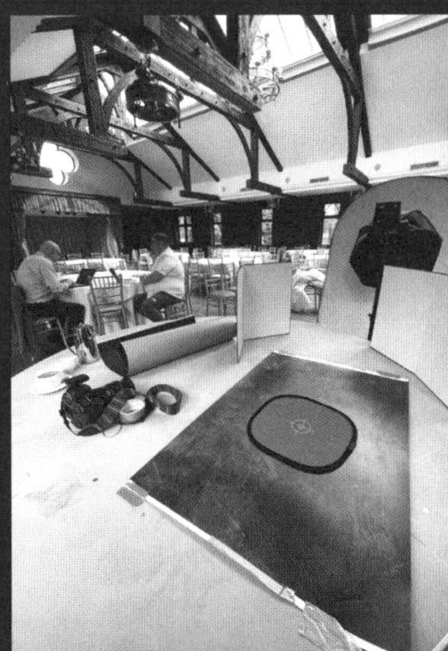

GANDOLFI COOKBOOK

Gideon Robinson & The Living Kitchen

The kitchen has always been a special place in our home, memories from childhood of sitting around a kitchen table, picking herbs from outside the back door, cooking with and for family and friends. The lounge and dining room always seemed distant cousins only to be visited on occasion.

Over my years in the kitchen industry there is a definite shift, people are reconsidering how they want to live in their space. Walls are coming away; lounges, dining rooms and kitchens are being combined more and more into one large living space, The Living Kitchen. This new space is now the hub of the home and is a backdrop to the ebbs and flow of family life, its emotions and its growth.

Scale is not so important within The Living Kitchen, whilst large rooms offer more opportunity; even small rooms can be remodelled to embrace the concept of The Living Kitchen. As long as you have considered function and flow then it is possible to introduce areas where people can sit, have a glass of wine or a chat while food is prepared.

The Living Kitchen is a social place, as well as providing sustenance, you should be able to relax, read a book or enjoy a coffee. At Gideon Robinson this is our philosophy.

Gideon and Susan have been designing and supplying Living Kitchens throughout Glasgow and beyond since they opened their first showroom in Glasgow in 2003. For up to date information **gideonrobinson.com**

What can Gideon Robinson do for you?

home@gideonrobinson.com

At Gideon Robinson we pride ourselves on listening. We listen to understand your requirements and wishes. We then work with you to develop a design that functions for you and for those who are going to be sharing your space.

The design of each kitchen can be broken down into a list of ingredients, no two kitchens are created using the same ingredients, we design to order! A form of slow cooking if you like. With access to a huge range of ingredients from cabinets and worktops to appliances and sinks, not forgetting the whole range of other accessories and finishes to add further individuality. The variety is without limit.

"Fantastic service, quality and workmanship"

★★★★★ Rated excellent on ★ Trustpilot

We all have slightly differing tastes and no two palettes are the same. As your personal kitchen designers we will work together with you to find the right combination of ingredients to match your palette. We may challenge you with some elements and surprise you with others. All the various elements should combine harmoniously to create the kitchen that delivers the same emotional response from tasting that wonderful slow cooked dish.

Gideon Robinson can take your ideas from concept to design and through to completion using our own in-house installers and working with approved contractors we can manage the whole process.

Whatever room you are looking at, be it the kitchen, the bedroom, a living or dining room or even a home office it will benefit from great design.

Gideon Robinson

CHAMPAGNE
PIAFF

PASTA

Contents

01

Swadish

Ajay Kumar
Owner

“We combine the best of Scottish food while taking pride in our Indian heritage.”

In 2003 I enrolled in cookery school and then worked in a whole assortment of different kitchens from India to Singapore and then to the UK. My journey brought me to Scotland in 2009 where I arrived in Edinburgh before moving to Glasgow in 2016. My dream was always having my own restaurant where I would have the freedom to cook my way. Glasgow was the perfect place for this to come true.

Swadish by Ajay Kumar takes the best of Scotland's amazing produce – Scotch beef, lamb, seafood, even exotic vegetables – and fuses it with the best of Indian spices. Scotland has some of the sweetest langoustines, oysters and scallops. We combine the finest of Scottish produce while taking pride in our Indian heritage.

I believe passionately in both seasonality and sustainability. That's why I focus on local suppliers to get the best quality for our customers. Some Scottish produce – which for me is the best in the world – such as lamb, venison and other game meats combines well with Indian flavours.

Our spices are sourced from the best suppliers, are ground and roasted to pair with each individual protein as we believe they all have different combinations of spices to make the dish special. This is how we surprise our customers' expectations and invite them to experience Indian cuisine in an innovative style.

I appeared in the popular Great British Menu BBC show and won for Scotland; it was an honour to represent us at the finals. Swadish currently holds 2 AA Rosettes for culinary excellence. We also attended the British Curry Awards as well as the Scottish Entertainments and Hospitality Awards and won Scotland's best Indian restaurant. It was a great experience to be the Scottish curry championship winner in 2018 as well.

I love to share all I have learned and began this part of my journey through the Covid lockdown when we started posting our cooking videos from home. This has built up a huge following of 280,000 people across the globe. We often get customers coming to Swadish from, London, Canada or the US requesting to meet me as they come after seeing my posts and clips on Facebook. It's an indescribable feeling to know that I have reached people far and wide who love to cook my recipes.

I would say being both the owner and head chef at Swadish by Ajay Kumar is one of the best jobs you could ever have as you are part of people's best moments and you're giving them a memorable time. People creating memories in my restaurant gives me a huge amount of satisfaction.

I love Glasgow; the people and the banter are brilliant, and I feel I'm an adopted son of the city. It's a privilege and an honour to be the owner and head chef of a restaurant like Swadish by Ajay Kumar in Glasgow.

Kerala prawn roast

Serves 4

Ingredients

King prawns - 500g. Cleaned and deveined

Sliced shallots - 15

Sliced and peeled cloves of garlic - 12

Fresh curry leaves - 20

Coriander powder - 2 tbsp

Mild red chilli powder - 2 tbsp

Turmeric powder - 1 tbsp

Cracked black pepper - 2 tsp

Oil for frying

Salt to taste

Method

Clean and devein the prawns. Rinse them well and drain thoroughly. Set aside.

Combine half of the powdered spices, the coriander powder, red chilli powder, turmeric powder, and salt.

Add the prawns to this spice mixture and mix well to ensure the prawns are evenly coated. Allow the prawns to marinate for at least 15 – 20 mins to absorb the flavours.

Heat a generous amount of oil in a large pan or kadai over medium heat. Add prawns and toss for 3 – 4 mins and remove from the pan.

Add the sliced shallots in the same pan and sauté them until they become light golden brown (top up oil if you need to before adding shallots). Add the garlic, curry leaves and continue sautéing until it is fragrant and lightly browned.

Once the shallots, garlic, and curry leaves are well-cooked, add the rest of the powdered spices and cook for 1 min on medium low flame.

Add prawns back into the pan and cook medium heat, stirring occasionally, until they turn pink and are cooked through, which should take about 3 – 4 mins. Stir frequently to prevent burning.

Once the prawn roast is ready, remove it from the heat.

Serve hot as a side dish with steamed rice, appam, or any Indian bread.

< Kerala prawn roast

Page 20 Kashmiri lamb rogan josh

Punjabi tandoori chicken

Ingredients

First stage marination

Skinless chicken thighs/breast - 640g

Ginger and garlic paste - 2 tbsp

Kashmiri red chili powder - 1 tsp

Lemon - 1/2 lemon for juice

Salt - 1 tsp

Second stage marination

Mustard oil - 3 tbsp

Kashmiri red chili powder - 2 tsp

Plain Greek-style yogurt - 2 tbsp

Ginger and garlic paste - 1 tbsp

Cumin powder - 1 tsp

Chaat masala - 1 tsp

Coriander powder - 1 tbsp

Dry kasoori methi (fenugreek leaves) - 1 tsp

Black salt - 1 tsp

Roasted gram flour - 1/2 tbsp

Unsalted, melted butter for basting

Salt to taste

Method

Serves 4

Apply first stage marinade onto chicken thighs and keep in fridge for 30 mins.

In a bowl, mix second stage ingredients and apply this mixture all over the chicken. Keep in fridge for 30 mins.

Preheat your grill or oven to 220°C.

Cook the chicken on the grill or in the oven for 10 mins until slightly charred.

Now, bring the oven temperature down to 170°C and cook chicken tikka until cooked through and juices run clear. (It should take approximately 15 – 20 mins depending on type and size for chicken). Baste the chicken with melted butter every 10 mins during cooking.

Remove the chicken from the grill or oven and let it rest for a few mins.

Serve hot with mint chutney, raita and lemon wedges.

< Punjabi tandoori chicken

Page 21 Alphonso mango kulfi

Kashmiri lamb rogan josh

Ingredients

Lamb - 500g. With or without bones
Mustard oil - 4 tbsp
Green cardamoms - 4-5
Cloves - 3-4
Plain yogurt - 1 cup
Kashmiri chili powder - 2 tsp
Dried ginger powder - 1 tsp
Dried mango powder - 1 tbsp
Fennel powder - 2 tsp
Asafoetida - 1/4 tsp
Lamb stock - 3 cups
Saffron - 1 pinch. Soaked in 2 tbsp warm water
Salt to taste

Method

Serves 4

Get your local butcher to cut 2 lamb shanks into a few pieces.

Heat the mustard oil in a heavy-bottomed pot over medium heat until it starts to smoke slightly. Reduce the heat to medium-low.

Add the green cardamoms and cloves, sautéing them until they release their aroma.

Add the lamb pieces to the pot, searing them on all sides until browned.

Set the flame setting to lowest and stir in chilli powder, ginger powder and fennel powder. Cook the spices for 1 min. Splash water to stop burning of powdered spices if necessary.

Pour in the lamb stock, stirring well to combine the ingredients.

Cover the pan with a lid and cook lamb for 30 – 40 mins on a low flame setting. Stir intermittently.

Now, add the well beaten yogurt and soaked saffron along with the liquid. Stir to evenly distribute the saffron.

Reduce the heat to low, cover the pot, and let the lamb simmer gently for 45 mins or until tender, stirring occasionally.

Cook until the lamb is cooked and the sauce has thickened to your desired consistency. The oil should begin to separate from the gravy.

Taste and adjust seasoning if needed.

Once the lamb is fully cooked and the sauce is rich and flavourful, remove from heat.

Serve the Lamb Rogan Josh hot, garnished with fresh ginger and coriander, alongside steamed basmati rice or naan.

Alphonso mango kulfi

Ingredients

Alphonso mangoes - 5. Or 425g mango puree

Double cream - 2 1/4 cups

Condensed milk - 195g

Citric acid granules - 1/4 tsp. Food grade

Powdered green cardamom seeds - 1/4 tsp

Saffron - 10 strands. Good quality

Salt - 1 pinch

Method

Soak saffron strands in 3 tbsp warm milk and let it bloom.

Peel mangoes and puree the flesh in a blender jar. Now, mix this puree with the double cream and blitz in a food processor until thickens but still of a pouring consistency (or just use a balloon whisk). Do not over whisk, it might split.

Put it in a mixing bowl and stir in citric acid granules, cardamom powder, saffron and salt.

Mix it well with the help of a spoon or silicon spatula. Pour it in silicon moulds of your choice and freeze overnight covered with cling film.

Demould when ready and let it soften to room temperature.

Serve with fresh fruits of your choice.

02 Ox And Finch
Aurelien Mourez
Head chef

I come from France and a family of winegrowers. People who are close to agriculture. As a teenager I was looking for something where I could be creative and that brought me to cooking because I could explore a world of food.

Ox And Finch is best described as casual dining. Over the years we've tried to have fresh approaches to classical dishes as well as inspiration for new ideas although we never limit ourselves to any one type of food or region. We strive to be simple and approachable in the best way we can. Ox And Finch is very much a collaborative effort.

All the chefs are encouraged to collaborate and participate in creating dishes. We work together on ideas and often fine tune the outcome of a dish with a fresh approach. We get the best results that way.

We also try not to overcomplicate things and ensure each plate has just the right number of elements in it. Our aim is to get inspiration by infusing classic dishes with new ingredients, simple but sophisticated. We've had ten years now to refine that.

I was twenty-one when I first moved to Glasgow, I barely spoke a word of English and put myself in a difficult situation, but I believe that's what helped me. The Glasgow accent didn't hinder me too much because my first experience of speaking English was through a Scottish or Glasgow accent; it became native to me in a way. Like a lot of my friends about ten-to-fifteen years ago, I could have gone to London, but they often ended up in restaurants headed by French chefs and the kitchen language, therefore, would be French, so you would end up hanging about with French people in London and not learning as much English. So, while it was difficult learning a new language on the job, once I became familiar with it, I was able to progress quickly from roles such as pastry chef to sous chef and eventually head chef.

I learned not to be afraid of taking a challenge. I realised that no matter how difficult things are it can only make you better. The harder you work, the bigger your progression.

Glasgow has its challenges like everywhere else. Ox And Finch has a large team, and we try to manage the sensibilities of everyone in that team so I make every effort to find out what makes each individual tick, what would help that individual to progress. There's a huge difference between learning the techniques and then going on to be the one who's teaching those skills and techniques. I didn't really anticipate that big difference.

The evolution of the food scene in Glasgow has been remarkable. When I began in the city thirteen years ago, there was much of a sameness and everyone in the trade was broadly doing the same thing. Now there's so much more creative people around in the city's dining scene. Glasgow, in terms of both its restaurants and its customers is open to new ideas and concepts around cuisine which is very healthy, and I firmly believe that Ox And Finch has been in the forefront of that.

“Infusing classic dishes with new ingredients, simple but sophisticated”

Beef tartare, horseradish and egg yolk purée

Ingredients

Egg yolk purée

Egg yolks - 4

Salt - 1g

Sherry vinegar - 2ml

Water - 5ml

Disposable piping bag - 1

Mustard dressing

Dijon mustard - 10g

Worcestershire sauce - 10ml

Chardonnay vinegar - 5ml

Pomace oil - 80ml

Salt - 1g

Beef tartare

Piece of beef - 500g. All fat and sinew removed (heart of rump, sirloin or fillet works well)

Lilliput capers - 20g

Shallots - 40g. Finely chopped

Cornichons - 40g. Finely chopped

Chives - 20g. Finely chopped

Mustard dressing

Batch of egg yolk purée

Sourdough bread - 200g. Torn into chunks

Melted butter - 50g

Mizuna leaves - 20g. Rocket, watercress or mustard greens can be used alternatively

Horseradish - 50g

Flaked sea salt and black pepper

Method

Serves 4

Egg yolk purée In the restaurant, we cook the egg yolk in a water bath at 72°C for 45 mins. At home with no water bath available, add the beaten egg yolks and the water to a heat proof bowl and cook over a pot of just simmering water, without the base of the bowl touching the water. Slowly heat, stirring constantly until thick and glossy.

If you have a thermometer or temperature probe at home, turn off the heat when the mixture reaches 72°C. Add salt and sherry vinegar and whisk together until smooth.

Roll down the edges of the piping bag so that you can easily get the egg yolk puree down into the tip. Transfer the egg yolk to the piping bag, tie the bag in a knot and trim off any excess, store in the fridge until required.

Mustard dressing In a bowl, whisk mustard, salt, Worcestershire sauce and vinegar together. Slowly trickle in the oil to emulsify while whisking continuously.

Beef tartare In a very hot pan, sear the beef on all sides and then remove and cool down immediately. Keep in the fridge until needed.

To make the croutons place the chunks of sourdough bread in a baking tray and coat in the melted butter. Cook in the oven at 200°C until golden brown and crispy all the way through. Season the finished croutons with salt.

To prepare the beef, carefully trim away all the seared part of the meat and discard this. Dice the remaining beef rump into 0.5cm cubes and put into a large, chilled bowl, add in the shallots, cornichons, chives, capers and mustard dressing. Add sea salt and freshly ground black pepper to taste and mix well. Spread the tartare on a plate and then top with dots of egg yolk purée, sprinkle over the croutons and salad leaves, and grate the fresh horseradish over top.

< Beef tartare, horseradish and egg yolk purée

Page 28 Pork fillet, ham hough butterbeans and parsley sauce

Smoked mackerel tonnato, tomato, peas and green beans

Ingredients

Tonnato

Smoked mackerel - 75g. Skin and bones removed

Extra virgin olive oil - 85ml

Pomace oil - 65ml

Garlic cloves - 25g. Peeled

Fresh lemon juice - 12ml

Zest of 1/4 of a lemon

Chardonnay vinegar - 6ml

Egg yolks - 2

Salt - 1g

Vinaigrette

Dijon mustard - 12g

Soy sauce - 5ml

Red wine vinegar - 10ml

Pomace oil - 90ml

Salt - 1g

To serve

Heritage tomatoes - 6 – 8. Cut into chunks

Green beans - 120g. Blanched in salted water and cooled

Fresh peas - 60g. Raw

Shallots - 40g. Finely chopped

Urfa pepper - 10g

Chervil - 8g

Basil - 12g

Flaked sea salt

Method

Serves 4

Tonnato Place the peeled garlic cloves into a small pan and cover with cold water, bring to the boil and simmer for 10 mins until soft.

In a blender, combine the blanched garlic, egg yolks, vinegar and salt and start to blend. In a jug, mix together the olive oil and pomace oil, then with the blender running, slowly start to add the oil to the egg mixture until emulsified.

Add the smoked mackerel to the blender and combine until smooth. Lastly, add the salt, lemon zest and juice.

Vinaigrette In a large bowl, whisk the mustard, salt, soy sauce and vinegar together. Slowly trickle the oil into the bowl while still whisking to combine.

To serve In a large bowl, add the tomatoes, green beans, peas, shallots, and 100ml of the vinaigrette. Add the salt and mix to combine.

Spread 2 tbsp of the tonnato onto each plate, and top with the tomato salad.

Garnish with picked chervil and basil leaves, and a sprinkle of urfa pepper.

< Smoked mackerel tonnato, tomato, peas and green beans

Page 29 Bare Bones Guatemala chocolate mousse, toasted rice and hazelnut

Pork fillet, ham hough butterbeans and parsley sauce

Ingredients

Pork fillet

Pork fillet steaks - 4 x 150g

Cold water - 2l

Table salt - 100g

Caster sugar - 100g

Parsley sauce

Shallots - 3. Thinly sliced

White wine - 250ml

Cream - 500ml

Flat leaf parsley - 150g. Stalks and leaves separated

Bay leaf - 1/2

Garlic clove - 1. Thinly sliced

Black peppercorns - 2g

Salt - 2g

Ham hough butterbeans

Smoked ham hough - 1. 800g – 1kg

Dried butterbeans - 500g

Salt - 5g

Garlic cloves - 4 – 5. Large

Small onion - 1. Peeled and halved

Carrot - 1. Peeled and halved

Celery stick - 1

Bay leaf - 1

Thyme - 4 – 5 sprigs

Cloves - 1g

Juniper - 2g

Coriander seeds - 2g

Black peppercorns - 2g

Method

Serves 4

Pork fillet To make the brine place the salt, sugar and water in a large container and whisk until the salt and sugar have dissolved. Submerge the pork fillets in the brine and refrigerate for an hour. Remove the pork from the brine and pat dry.

Parsley sauce Add the shallots and garlic to a frying pan and sweat in oil until soft. Add the white wine and reduce by half. Once reduced, add the cream, bay leaf, whole peppercorns and parsley stalks and simmer for 10 – 15 mins.

Remove the bay leaf, peppercorns and parsley stalks and add the mixture to a blender with the parsley leaves and blend until smooth.

Pass the mixture through a fine mesh sieve. Your sauce should be a vibrant green. Check for seasoning, adding more salt to taste.

Ham hough butterbeans Soak the butterbeans in water for a minimum of 4 hours before cooking, or overnight if possible.

Tie the thyme, bay leaf and whole spices together in a piece of muslin cloth.

Drain and rinse the soaked beans, and place them in a casserole dish along with the ham hough and the rest of the ingredients. Cover with hot water and cook in the oven for 3.5 – 4 hours at 200°C or until the ham and beans are fork tender.

Remove from the oven and allow to cool slightly before straining, make sure to reserve the cooking liquid. Remove the muslin, garlic, carrot, onion and celery. Pick all of the meat from the ham hough, add back to the beans with a ladle or two or the stock just to moisten. You can keep the leftover stock for a soup.

To serve In a frying pan, melt a generous nob of butter until foaming. Add the pork to the pan, and cook for 3 – 4 mins on each side, spooning the butter over the pork occasionally. Remove from the pan and let rest on a cutting board for 10 mins. While the pork is resting, gently warm up the parsley sauce and the ham hough beans in two separate pans.

To plate, place the beans and ham hough into the bottom of a plate or wide bowl. Carve the pork fillets into slices and serve on top of the beans. Spoon the parsley sauce over the top.

Bare Bones Guatemala chocolate mousse, toasted rice and hazelnut

Serves 4

Ingredients

Cocoa husk powder

Bare Bones chocolate husks - 50g

Icing sugar - 140g

Chocolate gavotte (shards)

Egg white - 30g

Icing sugar - 60g

Water - 125ml

Butter - 12g

Flour - 12g

Salt - 1g

Dark chocolate - 25g

Bare Bones chocolate husks - 25g

Toasted rice custard

Double cream - 250ml

Sugar - 65g

Egg yolks - 90g. Beaten

Jasmine rice - 55g

Gelatine leaf - 1. Soaked in cold water

Toasted hazelnuts

Blanched hazelnuts - 60g

Chocolate mousse

Guatemala 65% chocolate - 180g. Finely chopped

Milk chocolate - 75g

Milk - 75ml

Double cream - 125ml

Eggs - 3. Separated

Sugar - 20g

Method

Cocoa husk powder Cocoa husks are a rarely used by-product of the chocolate making industry. Bare Bones is an artisan, small batch chocolate maker based in Glasgow. They roast and process their cocoa beans so have plenty of husks to spare. Using this product, which normally goes to waste, adds a bit of bitterness to the flavour of the roasting process.

Simply blend them together in a food processor or spice grinder to a fine powder with the icing sugar.

Chocolate gavotte Gently melt the dark chocolate in a bowl over a pot of just simmering water, without the base of the bowl touching the water. Add the melted chocolate and the rest of the ingredients to a blender or food processor and mix on high until smooth.

Spread onto a baking sheet lined with parchment or a silicon mat in a thin layer. Bake in the oven at 170°C for 12 mins. Leave to cool and break into large, rough shards.

Toasted rice custard In a dry frying pan, toast the jasmine rice grains over a medium heat, moving frequently, until a pale golden brown. They can catch quickly, so be careful not to burn them. Set aside and allow to cool.

In a bowl whisk together the egg yolks, sugar, cooled rice and cream. Transfer to a saucepan, gently heat the mixture over a low heat, stirring continuously until it starts to steam. Add the gelatine leaf stirring until it has melted. Keep stirring over heat until the mixture is thickened, coating the back of a spoon. Pass the mixture through a fine mesh sieve, discarding the rice and any lumps. Divide between four dariole moulds and chill in the fridge to set.

Toasted hazelnuts Place the hazelnuts on a baking tray and roast in an oven at 200°C until golden brown, this should take around 8 mins. Remove from the oven, allow to cool slightly and crush into coarse chunks.

Chocolate Mousse In a small saucepan, bring the cream and milk to the boil. Add the chopped chocolate to a large bowl and pour in the hot cream and milk, stirring until combined. Add the egg yolks and stir to incorporate. Set the bowl aside and leave to cool at room temperature.

Use a stand or handheld mixer to whip the egg whites until they form soft peaks. Gradually add the sugar 2 tbsp at a time, continuing to whip until all the sugar is combined and the mixture is glossy, forming stiff peaks.

Add a quarter of the meringue to the cooled chocolate and stir to combine. Gently fold in the rest of the meringue being careful not to beat out the air. Transfer the mixture to a tub and refrigerate for 4 hours or until it is firmly set.

To serve Loosen the set custards from the moulds and turn out onto a plate. Add a scoop of the chocolate mousse on top of the custard, sprinkle over the toasted hazelnuts. Decorate with the chocolate shards and dust with chocolate husk powder.

03

Kelp
Christopher Hutchins
Head chef

"Scotland has the best larder in the world and that gives me a great palette to work a culinary canvas on."

I got the bug for hospitality from an early age. My dad, a chef, and mum owned a hotel and restaurant. During my summer holidays I started peeling potatoes and various other tasks in the kitchen. I went to university, but as soon as I could I was drawn to hospitality. For me it was such a creative outlet which I couldn't find anywhere else.

I worked in hotels and restaurants around the country, including hotels with two and three Rosettes before working in various restaurants in Glasgow including the Partick Duck Club and Six by Nico. This was all invaluable experience before I came to Kelp when it opened in 2022.

Kelp is a small plates sustainable Scottish seafood restaurant, focused on seasonality and Scottish produce. Scotland has the best larder in the world and that gives me a great palette to work a culinary canvas on. We use local suppliers with small supply chains such as the Fish People and the Tobermory Fish Company. We source our langoustines direct from Skye, and we're developing a herb garden outside the restaurant for fresh herbs to use in our cooking.

Our aim at Kelp is to take Scottish produce and marry it with influences from across the globe to create something distinctive and unusual. One of our signature dishes is crab donut which is very popular. Another staple dish is Basque cheesecake.

The emphasis on sustainability comes from the owner of Kelp, Neil Douglas, who's developed a strong ethos of sustainability.

I would say that my 'food philosophy' is to utilise the seasons and what's available, at its best and be creative. There are a lot of restaurants in Glasgow and Kelp is at the edge of the city centre. It's in a unique location, a beautiful space, and has its own garden and outdoor dining; something that you don't find in the city centre. I knew at the outset we needed to set ourselves apart from our peers and find a style which wasn't too challenging for our guests. I feel we've achieved that, gaining recognition from the Good Food Guide and AA along the way. That's something I'm very proud of.

One of the most challenging experiences I've had was working in a hotel restaurant in Yorkshire on a very busy night when we had a power cut. There was a foot-and-a-half of snow outside and we had to find ways of serving guests including using camping stoves, barbecues and anything that came to hand. We managed to serve everyone and turned a looming disaster into a positive experience by working together as a team. Yes, it was stressful, but we had fun.

What I learned from that is that the key is to keep the head and roll with the punches. Teamwork is vital to this. You should ensure everyone, from the kitchen porter to the head chef is involved and getting stuck in. I was very inspired by my father's approach to be being a chef which focused on keeping calm and meticulous while never expecting anyone to do something he wasn't prepared to do himself. I hope I've inherited those traits.

Being a chef in hospitality in Glasgow is very rewarding. People are warm, welcoming and make you feel part of the city. It helps that Kelp has an open kitchen which encourages diners to interact with you and provide great feedback.

It's a great city with fantastic attitude and a thriving cultural scene. Certainly, in the time I've been here I'm aware Glasgow people are more open to trying new dishes when they're dining out.

Confit pork belly al pastor

Ingredients

Pork belly

Pork belly - 1kg. Skinless & boneless
Oil (neutral veg or rapeseed)
Bay leaves - 4
Orange - 1. Quartered
Chipotle chilli - 1
Star anise - 2
Garlic bulb - 1. Cut in half
Salt

Al pastor

Chipotle in adobe - 1 tin
Guajillo chilli - 1g
Shallots - 1. Diced
Garlic cloves - 4. Minced
Oregano - 1/2 tbsp
Orange juice - 250ml
Passata - 250g
Coriander powder - 1 tsp
Soft dark brown sugar - 50g
Cider vinegar - 20g
Pineapple diced - 1
Pork stock - 100ml. Reduced

The kebab

Bamboo skewers - 6 inch skewers
Monkfish tails - 40g pieces.

Pineapple gel

Pineapple - 1. Diced
Sugar - 200g
Pineapple juice - 100ml

To plate

Micro coriander
Pork air bag
Sliced jalapeño

Method

Pork belly Place pork belly into a deep oven tray. Sprinkle with salt. Add the orange, chilli, star anise, and garlic and completely cover in oil, the pork belly should be fully submerged.

Cover with tin foil and place in a preheated oven at 130°C for 4 hours. Remove from the oven and allow to cool in the confit oil.

Once cooked place in a separate oven tray and place another weighted tray on top of the pork belly and press under weight overnight in the fridge.

Once pressed trim and cut into 4cm pieces and reserve.

Al pastor Sweat off shallots garlic and chilli over a medium heat. Add oregano and coriander. Add in the chipotle in adobe and cook out for 5 mins.

Add in the pork stock. Add in the Passata, orange juice, sugar, vinegar and pineapple. Turn down the heat and reduce by half.

Turn the mixture to a food processor and blend until smooth.

The kebab Get a 6 inch bamboo skewer and alternate between pork belly pieces cut earlier and 40g pieces of monkfish tail.

Pineapple gel In a pan bring all ingredients to a simmer and cook until soft. Allow to cool slightly and turn to a food processor and blitz to a purée.

To plate Sprinkle the skewer with pork air bag. Add a few slices of jalapeños and garnish with micro coriander.

Finish the plate with a rocher of pineapple gel.

< Confit pork belly al pastor

Page 36 Oysters with rhubarb and ginger mignonette

Shetland mussels, cider, chorizo broth, almond picada

Ingredients

Shetland mussels - 500g. Or 250g for a small portion

Cider chorizo broth

Onion - 1. Diced

Garlic cloves - 3. Minced

Chorizo - 1 x 250g ring. Diced

Fennel - 1 bulb

Chicken stock - 1l

Cider - 500ml

Chopped tomatoes - 2 x 400g tins

Soft dark brown sugar - 25g

Cider vinegar - 25ml

Smoked paprika - 2 tbsp

Almond picada

Micro coriander leaves - 100g

Perthshire rapeseed oil - 200ml

Almonds - 100g

Garlic cloves - 2

Sherry - 75ml

Sherry vinegar - 1 splash

Lemon - 1. Zested

Chilli flakes - 1 tsp

Salt to taste

Method

Cider chorizo broth Sweat off the onions, garlic and fennel. Add the smoked paprika. Then add the chorizo and cook out. Pour in the chicken stock, cider, and chopped tomatoes. Then add the sugar and vinegar. Cook for 30 mins over a medium heat until the chorizo is soft and falling apart.

Then use a stick blender to blend into a smooth broth.

Almond picada Add all ingredients to a food processor and blend together.

To plate Place a pan over a high heat and add 250g for a small portion or 500g for a larger portion of de-bearded and cleaned Shetland mussels. Add a splash of cider or white wine and cover.

Allow the mussels to steam open and remove from the heat.
In a separate pan warm the chorizo broth. When hot add the mussels to the pot and serve.

Spoon over the Picada and garnish with micro coriander.

< Shetland mussels, cider, chorizo broth, almond picada

Page 37 Burnt basque cheesecake

Oysters with rhubarb and ginger mignonette

Ingredients

Oysters - 12 – 16. We use Loch Fyne Oysters

The mignonette

Rhubarb - 100g
Pickled pink sushi ginger - 50g
Red wine vinegar - 200g
Caster sugar - 100g
Grenadine - 100g

Method

Peel and fine brunoise the rhubarb. Fine brunoise the ginger. Mix together the red wine vinegar, sugar and grenadine – stir until sugar dissolves. Add the brunoise rhubarb and ginger.

To plate First open the oysters. Wrap a towel over one hand and use it to hold the oyster firmly, ensure the oyster is flat side up. Using an oyster knife in the other hand, place the end of the blade at the base of the hinge, twist the knife using pressure, then lever the knife upwards and twist it to prise the hinge open. Slide the knife under the top shell to release the oyster. Use the knife to release the from it's shell, a small connective muscle found on the left side of the oyster shell. Then flip the oyster, spoon over the mignonette and serve over crushed ice.

Burnt basque cheesecake

Ingredients

Burnt basque cheesecake

Cream cheese - 1.4kg
Plain flour - 30g
Caster sugar - 400g
Vanilla - 50g
Eggs - 7
Double cream - 100g

Lemon curd

Unwaxed lemons - 2. Juice and zested
Caster sugar - 100g
Unsalted butter - 50g
Eggs - 2. Beaten

To plate

Fresh Scottish raspberries

Method

Burnt basque cheesecake All ingredients should be at room temperature. Place the cream cheese, sugar, vanilla, and flour in a stand mixer and beat together on the slowest speed for 10 mins. Scrape down the side of the mixing bowl every few mins. Gradually feather in the eggs one by one. Once combined, pour in the double cream and mix for another min.

Transfer to a lined 27cm spring form tin and cook in a pre heated oven at 200°C for 40 mins.

Lemon curd Put the lemon zest, juice, sugar and butter in a heatproof bowl over a pan of simmering water. Stir until the butter has melted. Then stir in the beaten egg, and gently whisk the mixture over the heat for around 10 mins until thickened like custard.

Once cooked pass through a fine sieve and reserve in the fridge for later.

To plate Place a slice of cheesecake on a plate. Add a spoonful of lemon curd, and finish with fresh Scottish raspberries.

04 Brett
Colin Anderson
Chef director

From a young age I'd been the family chef at home, cooking for my older brother and sister while mum was working full time. I taught myself simple recipes from my mum's cookbooks. My real introduction to hospitality started while working on a fishing boat during school holidays on the Isle of Colonsay in the Inner Hebrides of Scotland. I loved watching the fish being caught, landed, sorted then sold for the plate. My interest in what happened to the fish must have been quite obvious as the head chef from the Colonsay Hotel asked me to come and be his trainee for the summer after finishing my exams at school. I quickly knew this was the career for me.

On my 17th birthday I was taken to the famous Ubiquitous Chip in Glasgow and was blown away. I was determined to work there. After leaving Colonsay to return to Glasgow I secured a job as a commis chef. A role at the original Cail Bruich followed then a move to London, working at the 3 Michelin starred Restaurant Gordon Ramsay in Chelsea. Later I worked in fine dining restaurants in Australia before coming back to Glasgow.

Paul and Chris Charalambous, the owners of Cail Bruich, asked me to rejoin them. They were looking to open a new venture. Brett was born. It started out as a natural wine bar and organically evolved to the restaurant it is today.

Brett is a modern European style restaurant, styled on my idea of a restaurant I would like to dine in. We have an open kitchen where guests can view and absorb the cooking while interacting with the chefs. Our guests are part of the experience at Brett where they and the staff interact together to make a great ambiance enjoying beautifully cooked, high-quality food and great service in relaxed surroundings.

There is a great emphasis in dining today on sustainability, but at Brett we really do focus on minimising wastage which benefits the environment as well as adding something unique to the dishes. This could be in the form of a fermentation or infusion – always enhancing the flavour and often adding a twist, which can both surprise and delight our guests. We make use of classic sauces and love the harmony of balance between acidity, fat and texture.

We have developed a good teamwork ethos with a progressive and a healthy work/life balance for the team. By treating our staff well, we believe they will treat our guests in the best way. As we develop and improve, our team changes as they progress their careers. With each cycle of change there are difficulties with training new team members, but we embrace these changes and always aim to come out the cycle better. We aim to be 1% better every day. This is reflected in the reviews we have had from the national press and the feedback from our guests.

I believe we have created a great vibe in the restaurant. This is largely because we endeavour to create a memorable experience for our guests and by joining them on their journey rather than just serving them.

“Our guests, are part of the experience at Brett...enjoying beautifully cooked, high-quality food.”

Haggis, neeps and tatties a'la Brett

Ingredients

Haggis

Lamb pluck (heart, lungs & liver) - 1.4kg
Lamb mince - 500g
Unsalted butter - 150g
Lamb stock - 2l
Suet - 200g
Pinhead oatmeal - 500g. Toasted
Onion - 250g. Finely chopped
Garlic cloves - 4
Black pepper - 1 tbsp
White pepper - 1 tbsp
Long peppers - 8
Ground nutmeg - 1 tsp
Ground cloves - 1 tsp
Coriander seeds - 4 tsp
Pimento - 2 tbsp
Dried wakame - 2 tbsp
Dried shiitake - 50g

Haggis & potato ballotines

Haggis - 240g
Chicken breast - 100g
Cream - 40g
Egg white - 20g
Large Maris Piper potato - 1. Peeled

Method

Serves 4

Haggis Dice the pluck into roughly 5cm dice and season evenly with fine salt. Heat a large sauce pan over a high heat and add some neutral oil. Fry the lamb pluck dice until nice and caramelised. Add the butter and cook until browned.

De-glaze the pan with 100ml of water to remove any caramelisation from the bottom of the pan. Add the lamb stock and bring to a simmer. Cook for around 2 hours. Topping the stock up with water as necessary to make sure the pluck is covered with liquid.

Remove from the heat and allow to cool to around 50°C. Strain the stock and reserve. Put the pluck through a course mincer.

Season your lamb mince evenly with fine salt. In a large saucepan on a high heat brown the lamb mince, mixing regularly to separate the grains. Remove the mince from the pan. In the same pan on a medium heat, sweat the onion and garlic with a little fine salt, cooking until very soft.

Meanwhile in a dry pan, toast the peppers, cloves, coriander and pimento. Combine with dried wakame and shiitake and grind in a spice grinder. Add spice mix to the sweated onions and garlic and cook for 3 mins on a low heat.

Add stock from cooking the lamb pluck and the minced pluck. Simmer this on a low heat for around two hours.

Meanwhile preheat the oven to 180°C and put the pinhead oatmeal on a tray and toast until dark golden brown. After the haggis mix has been cooking for two hours and most of the liquid has been cooked out, add your toasted oatmeal and cook for a further 15 mins.

Add the suet and cook for a further 5 mins. Check seasoning, add salt as necessary. If you like your haggis more spiced then, feel free to add some more toasted ground pepper at this stage. Cool the haggis completely and reserve.

Haggis & potato ballotines In a food processor, pulse the chicken until finely chopped. Add the egg white and pulse until blended. With the machine on, add the cream in a steady stream and purée until smooth.

Scrape the mousse into a bowl and stir in the haggis. Weigh the mix into 85g sausage shapes and roll tightly into a ballotine with cling film, tie each end tightly. Cook in simmering water for 10 mins. Refresh in ice water.

Using a Japanese mandolin turn the potato into spaghetti shaped ribbons. Blanch in boiling water for 30 secs then refresh in ice water. Remove from the ice water and dry well.

Ingredients

"Auld Alliance" haggis sauce

Shallots - 150g. Sliced

Lamb trim - 500g. Diced

Garlic - 3 cloves. Cut in half

Thyme - 1 sprig

Black peppercorns - 4

Sea salt - 2g

Sherry vinegar - 50ml

Veal stock - 1.5l

Lamb stock - 1.5l

Highland Park 12 Y/O whisky - 100ml

Double cream - 200 ml

Fatty duck liver (diced) - 100g

Pickled turnips

Small Turnip (Scottish neep) - 1

Saffron - 1/2 g

Rice wine vinegar - 250ml

Sugar - 180g

Water - 75ml

Pomme purée

Lovers choice potatoes - 500g. Washed

Double cream - 100g

Milk - 50g

Butter - 100g. Diced at room temperature

Salt

Remove the haggis from the cling film carefully and wrap the potato neatly around each haggis ballotine. Reserve these in the fridge.

"Auld Alliance" haggis sauce In a large sauce pan on a high heat, fry off the lamb trim in oil, getting to golden brown stage then remove from pan. In the same pan, on a medium heat, fry and sweat shallots until coloured and soft. Add thyme, salt, peppercorns, garlic and cook for a further 2 mins.

Push shallots etc aside and de-glaze pan with 1/2 of the vinegar - letting the heat do the work. Move the shallots across to the other side of the pan and de-glaze the rest of the pan, making sure the bottom of the pan is completely free of any caramelisation.

Add pork trim back into the pan. Add stocks and bring to the boil and skim off any impurities as you go. Simmer for about 2 hours until infusion tastes good. Strain with colander and reduce by 1/2.

In a new pan fry the fatty duck liver until caramelised on the outside. Remove the liver from the pan. De-glaze the pan with the whisky then add your lamb sauce and cream. Reduce this for 5 mins.

Add the duck liver and blend in a food processor until smooth. Pass through a fine mesh sieve. Season with salt and some more sherry vinegar if necessary.

Pickled turnips Bring everything to a boil and infuse saffron overnight. Meanwhile peel the turnip and cut into rectangle pieces at around 6cm wide. Using a mandolin, shave thin strips off the turnip.

Strain the saffron and discard then reboil the pickle liquid. Pour hot over shaved turnip to cover. Leave at least overnight to pickle.

Pomme purée Bake the potatoes on a bed of salt in the oven at 200°C until tender. Check with a small knife. Let rest for 10 mins out the oven with a dish cloth on top.

Meanwhile heat the cream and milk in a saucepan.

Push the potatoes through a drum sieve without working the potatoes too much as this will stretch the starch and give a waxy mashed potato. Put the potatoes into a pan and add the hot milk and cream and the room temperature butter. Mix well and season with salt.

Pass through a fine mesh drum sieve. Keep warm.

Contd. on next page >

Haggis, neeps and tatties a'la Brett (contd.)

Ingredients

Brett brown sauce

Pitted dates - 250g

Water - 500g

Sherry vinegar - 150ml

Crispy lamb sweetbreads

Lamb sweetbreads - 300g. Outer sinew removed

Chicken stock - 100g

Fine salt - 4g

Corn flour - 100g

Smoked paprika - 10g

To finish

Haggis ballotines - 4

Lamb sweetbread - 4. Flour coated pieces at 80g

Brett brown sauce

Pomme purée

Pickled neeps

Auld Alliance haggis sauce

Method

Brett brown sauce In a medium saucepan on a medium heat cook your dates in the water until almost no water remains. Put the dates into a food processor and blend until smooth. Add the sherry vinegar and blend further. Pass through a fine mesh sieve. Reserve in a squeeze bottle and keep warm.

Crispy lamb sweetbreads Dissolve salt in chicken stock. Put sweetbreads into a vacuum pack bag with salted chicken stock. Cook in a water bath at 65°C for 20 mins. Cool in an ice bath then remove the sweetbreads from bags and dry using kitchen towel. Mix the corn flour and paprika and dip the sweetbreads into the flour mix.

To finish Preheat your deep frier oil to 180°C then add your haggis balllotines and sweetbreads.

Meanwhile warm your pomme puree in a small pan.

Warm your neeps in a small pan. And warm your Auld Alliance haggis sauce in a pan being careful not to boil as the fat from the liver will split out if it boils.

On a hot plate put a dollop of brown sauce, a spoon of pomme puree and a pinch of pickled neeps.

Remove the ends of the haggis and carve in half so you have 2 cylinders.

Put the crispy sweetbreads on the plate.

Sauce generously.

Scallop cooked in the shell with its own consomme and finger lime

Ingredients

Scallops - 4. XL hand dived Scottish scallops in the shell

Coral butter

Unsalted butter - 250g

Scallop corals - 100g. Dehydrated

Fish broth base

Shallots - 100g. Peeled and halved

Garlic - 2 cloves

Unsalted butter - 100g

Rice wine vinegar - 100ml

Chicken stock - 2l

Water - 2l

Chicken wings - 1kg

Dried wakame - 50g

Dried mushrooms - 25g

Scallop skirts - 50g. Cleaned and dried

Mussels - 250g. Washed

Method

Serves 4

Scallops Dice the pluck into roughly 5cm dice and season evenly with fine salt. We use hand dived scallops for environmental reasons and for quality reasons.

To shuck your scallop, take a boning knife and insert it close to where the 2 shells join. Angle the knife towards the flat shell and slice all the way down between the shells in one motion. The idea is to leave no scallop meat on the flat shell so it is important the knife is pushing hard against the flat shell.

Make an incision between the scallop and the white muscle which will release the scallop from the shell. Keep the orange corals and translucent skirt separate. Keep the rounded shell as we'll serve the scallop in this.

Wash the scallops well with cold water and dry well using some kitchen cloth. Now wash the corals in the same way as the scallops.

To wash the skirts place under running cold water with a sieve on top to stop them floating away. Leave them under the water for about 20 mins, during this time use your hands to agitate and move the skirts around 4 times.

The skirts should be much more translucent white now. Dehydrate the skirts and corals separately in a fan oven at 80°C for a few hours. Make sure they are completely dry before removing and storing in an airtight container until using later.

Coral butter Put the butter in a medium saucepan over a medium high heat and allow it to melt.

Meanwhile blitz the corals to a powder.

Caramelise and foam the butter until it smells sweet and nutty. Pass through a fine mesh sieve. Add the coral powder and mix well. Keep this somewhere warm for an hour mixing regularly. Pass through a fine mesh sieve.

Fish broth base Sweat shallots, garlic, onion in butter with no colour. Add vinegar and reduce to compot so there is almost no liquid left. Add stock, water and wings, simmer for 2 hours.

Add wakame, scallop skirts, mussels and mushrooms. Bring to boil and cook for 10 mins on the boil. Rest for 1 hour and pass through a fine mesh sieve into the pan which you will use later to clarify in.

Allow to cool over night, this allows the fat to settle on the top of the stock.

Ingredients

Raft for clarifying

Chicken breast - 100g

Carrot - 50g. Peeled and chopped

Fennel - 50g. Herb removed

Onion - 50g. Peeled and diced

Scallop skirts - 50g. Cleaned and dried

Egg whites - 6

To finish

Scallops - 4. Shucked and dried

Coral butter - 100g

Scallop consomme - 100ml

Finger lime pearls - 20g

Scallop shells - 4. Well cleaned

Course sea salt

Raft for clarifying Skim all the fat off the top of the stock which has formed overnight. To make the raft place all the ingredients in a blender and blend to a smooth paste.

Bring the stock up to 40°C in the pan then whisk in the raft. Continue to cook on a low heat, stirring carefully with a wooden spoon. Once the raft has reached simmering point – check there are no bits of the raft stuck to the bottom of the pan using the wooden spoon then don't stir again.

Allow the stock and raft to simmer for 20 mins. Remove from the heat and let rest for a further 20 mins.

Strain the clarified stock out using a ladle and a fine mesh sieve.

Bring the stock back to the boil in a new pan and skim any impurities off. Check the flavour and reduce slightly if necessary. Check seasoning.

To finish We find the best way to cook these scallops is in the shell over a BBQ but if you aren't lighting the BBQ then feel free to cook them in a non stick frying pan.

If you are cooking the scallops in the shells, you will need to season the shells to stop the scallop sticking. Half fill the shells with course sea salt and bake in the oven at 180°C for 45 mins. Allow to cool completely then discard the salt.

Put the shells directly into the hot coals of the BBQ and add 10g of the coral butter into each shell. Place the scallop in with the larger side (the one which was attached to the flat shell) down into the scallop. This will be the presentation side.

Using tongs make sure the butter is getting under the scallop by agitating it slightly every few seconds until its clear the scallops aren't sticking. Leave the scallops alone now for a couple of mins to cook.

Remove the shells and scallops from the BBQ and flip the scallops. Add the remaining coral butter to each shell and leave the scallops somewhere warm to rest in the butter. The residual heat of the butter and shell will finish cooking the scallop.

Meanwhile heat the scallop consomme in a small pan. Next discard almost all the coral butter from the scallop shells. Top up each shell with consomme.

Place a little course salt onto a plate and place the scallop shell on top. Carve the scallop in half and top with finger lime pearls.

Page 44 Scallop cooked in the shell with its own consomme and finger lime

> Mushroom XO linguini, Cantabrian anchovies, 36 month aged parmesan veloute...

Mushroom XO linguini, Cantabrian anchovies, 36 month aged parmesan veloute, crispy leeks

Ingredients

Pasta dough

'00' pasta flour - 250g
Egg yolks - 2
Whole eggs - 2
Olive oil - 5g
Fine salt - 2g

Method

Serves 4

Pasta dough Place the flour on a board or in a bowl. Make a well in the centre and crack the eggs into it. Beat the eggs with a fork until smooth. Using the tips of your fingers, mix the eggs with the flour, incorporating a little at a time, until everything is combined. Knead the pieces of dough together – with a bit of work and some love and attention they'll all bind together to give you one big, smooth lump of dough.

Once you've made your dough you need to knead and work it with your hands to develop the gluten in the flour, otherwise your pasta will be flabby and soft when you cook it, instead of springy and al dente. There's no secret to kneading. You just have to bash the dough about a bit with your hands, squashing it into the table, reshaping it, pulling it, stretching it, squashing it again. Stop when your pasta starts to feel smooth and silky instead of rough and floury.

Wrap the dough in cling film and put it in the fridge to rest for at least 30 mins – make sure the cling film covers it well or it will dry out.

To roll your pasta First of all, if you haven't got a pasta machine it's not the end of the world. All the Nonna's in Italy roll pasta with their trusty rolling pins and they wouldn't even consider having a pasta machine in the house. The main problem you'll have is getting the pasta thin enough to work with. The way around this is to roll lots of small pieces of pasta rather than a few big ones. You'll be rolling your pasta into a more circular shape than the long rectangular shapes you'll get from a machine.

If using a machine to roll your pasta, make sure it's clamped firmly to a clean work surface before you start (use the longest available work surface you have). Dust your work surface with some Tipo '00' flour, take a lump of pasta dough the size of a large orange and press it out flat with your fingertips. Set the pasta machine at its widest setting – and roll the lump of pasta dough through it. Lightly dust the pasta with flour if it sticks at all.

Click the machine down a setting and roll the pasta dough through again. Fold the pasta in half, click the pasta machine back up to the widest setting and roll the dough through again. Repeat this process five or six times. It might seem like you're getting nowhere, but in fact you're working the dough, and once you've folded it and fed it through the rollers a few times, you'll feel the difference. It'll be smooth as silk and this means you're making really good pasta.

Now it's time to roll the dough out properly, working it through all the settings on the machine, from the widest down to around the narrowest. Lightly dust both sides of the pasta with a little flour every time you run it through.

When you've got down to the narrowest setting, to give yourself a tidy sheet of pasta, fold the pasta in half lengthways, then in half again, then in half again once more until you've got a square-ish piece of dough. Turn it 90° and feed it through the machine at the widest setting. As you roll it down through the settings for the last time, you should end up with a lovely rectangular silky sheet of dough with straight sides.

Contd. on next page >

Mushroom XO linguini, Cantabrian anchovies, 36 month aged parmesan veloute, crispy leeks (contd.)

Ingredients

Crispy leeks

Leeks - 250g. Whites only

Table salt - 4% of the weight of leeks once sliced

Neutral oil for frying

Mushroom XO sauce

Boiling water - 1 litre

Dried shiitake - 10g

King oyster mushrooms - 100g

Neutral oil - 100g. Vegetable or light olive oil

Button mushrooms - 250g

Garlic peeled and chopped - 50g

Ginger peeled and chopped - 50g

Red chilli - 50g. Deseeded & chopped

Sherry vinegar - 50g

Soy sauce - 50g

Truffle paste - 50g. Optional

Whether you're rolling by hand or by machine you'll need to know when to stop. If you're making pasta like tagliatelle, lasagne or linguini you'll need to roll the pasta down to between the thickness of a beer mat and a playing card; if you're making a stuffed pasta like ravioli or tortellini, you'll need to roll it down slightly thinner or to the point where you can clearly see your hand or lines of newsprint through it. Once you've rolled your pasta the way you want it, you need to shape or cut it straight away. Pasta dries much quicker than you think, so whatever recipe you're doing, don't leave it more than a minute or two before cutting or shaping it. You can lay over a damp clean tea towel which will stop it from drying.

Crispy leeks Cut the leeks into 2 inch cylinders then cut in half long ways. Separate the layers of leek into piles of 3 – 4 layers. Finely slice the leek long ways into what chefs call fine julienne.

We use the greens and trimmings to make a mushroom and leek stock which we use for the parmesan sauce. Add salt to 4% of the total weight of sliced leeks.

Leave for 30 mins then wash off all the salt and squeeze dry using a dish cloth. No liquid should come out when you twist the towel round and squeeze as tightly as you can.

Once dry, deep fry the leeks at 180°C in neutral oil until light golden brown. Stir the leeks continuously to help the colouration be even.

The leeks will continue to colour for a few seconds after they have been removed from the oil.

Mushroom XO sauce Finely dice the king oyster mushrooms then add oil to a large frying pan and cook until golden brown. It's important to get a bit of umami rich colour on the mushrooms at this point.

Strain off using a sieve but reserve the oil and the pan as we'll be using it again shortly.

Place the chopped garlic, ginger and chillies in a food processor and blend on the pulse setting until it resembles a paste. You can finely chop everything but this makes life a little easier. Reserve this chilli paste.

Using the same food processor (there is no need to clean it as everything is going in together) blend the button mushrooms to create a mushroom paste. Reserve this too.

Add the oil back into the pan and add the chilli paste and a pinch of salt. Cook this on a medium heat for a few mins allowing the paste to soften and the flavour to mellow. Add the blended button mushrooms and the golden brown king oyster dice to the pan. Cook this for a few more mins.

Meanwhile dice the shiitake mushrooms which have been rehydrating in the water. You can add the diced shiitake back into the shiitake stock as both will be added at the same time a little later.

Once the mushroom and chilli mix in the pan has been simmering for a few mins, deglaze the bottom of the pan with sherry vinegar.

Ingredients

Mushroom & leek stock

Dried mushroom trim - 100g

Leek trimmings - washed - 200g

Water - 400ml

Veloute

Parmesan rind trim - as much as you have remaining

Sliced shallots - 50g

Dry vermouth - 50ml

Mushroom & leek stock - 250ml

Double cream - 250ml

Parmesan - 100g. Finely grated on a microplane

To finish

Rolled linguini - 400g

Mushroom XO sauce - 300g

Unsalted butter - 60g

Parmesan veloute

Crispy leeks - in 4 neat birds nest like piles

Cantabrian anchovies - 4

Add the shiitake stock, diced shiitake and soy sauce. Cook for around an hour on a low heat. Finish with optional black truffle paste. Check the seasoning.

Mushroom and leek stock Cover with water and bring to boil then simmer for 10 mins. Pass through a fine mesh sieve.

Veloute Sweat shallots with a pinch of salt in a small amount of oil until very soft. This is bringing out the sweetness of the shallot and taking away the harsh raw onion flavour.

Add the parmesan rind and cook a little longer but not so long that the parmesan rind starts to colour as this will add the flavour of toasted cheese to the sauce which we don't want.

Add the vermouth and reduce to compot where there is almost no liquid left at all. Add the mushroom and leek stock then reduce this by half. Add cream and bring back to the boil – simmer for 2 mins. Pass through a fine sieve.

Blend in the finely grated parmesan. Add more parmesan as necessary and adjust the seasoning with salt if necessary. If you question if it needs more parmesan – it definitely does.

To finish We use Ortiz anchovies and get the biggest plumpest ones available. Be sure to keep them in the oil until the last moment.

Have a pan of boiling water on the stove and your Parmesan sauce warm but never boiling. Meanwhile in another pan put your mushroom XO and gently heat it until it's just about to boil. Put your pasta into the boiling water and cook for 1 min. Agitate it gently as it goes into the water so it doesn't stick together.

Add your cooked pasta to the XO along with a little of the pasta cooking water and the butter.

Use the pan to toss the pasta through the XO and butter. The butter, XO and pasta water should form an emulsion which coats the pasta.

Using a carving fork roll the pasta against the pan into neat rolls and slide off onto the plate.

Divide the remaining XO emulsion between the portions then top with the anchovy and crispy leeks.

Using a hand blender, re blend the Parmesan sauce to form bubbles and scoop these onto the plate beside the pasta.

Apple tart tatin

Ingredients

Vanilla ice cream

Whole milk - 1l
Double cream - 325ml
Vanilla pods - 2
Egg yolks - 270g
Caster sugar - 155g
ProCrema ice cream stabiliser - 150g

Caramel sauce

Caster sugar - 300g
Double cream - 240g

Tatin

Caster sugar - 60g
Unsalted butter - 60g
Pink lady apples - 6
Puff pastry - 200g

Method

Serves 4

Vanilla ice cream Scrape the seeds from the vanilla pods and put the pods into a saucepan with the milk and cream. Bring the cream and milk to a simmer (not boil).

Meanwhile In a mixing bowl whisk the egg yolks sugar and vanilla seeds until pale. Pour hot milk and cream into yolks and sugar, whisking constantly.

Put the mix back into the pan and cook until it reaches 80°C. Allow to cool completely then add 150g ProCrema. If you can't get ProCrema then use another ice cream stabiliser with its instructions.

Pass through a fine sieve. Churn with your ice cream machine.

Caramel sauce In a saucepan bring sugar to a bronze caramel. Shock the caramel with cream. Be careful it will bubble and steam. Pass through a fine mesh sieve.

Tatin You should prepare your apples three days in advance doing this dries them out and intensifies the flavour but also stops so much liquid coming out and diluting the caramel.

Peel, quarter and core the apples. Dry for 3 days uncovered in the fridge. Don't worry if they go brown.

Once your apples are ready, bring sugar to a bronze caramel in the tatin pan. Add butter and allow to bubble. Allow to cool before adding dried apples. Arrange the apples round the pan, putting the peeled side down against the caramel. Put 18 pieces round the perimeter and the remaining 6 in the centre.

Roll out the puff pastry to 4mm thick and cut a circle the same size as the circumference of the pan.

Carefully tuck the pastry edges down the side of the apples, being sure to tuck under. Use a fork to make a few small holes in the pastry to let the steam out when cooking. Rest the tatin in the fridge for 20 mins.

Preheat the oven to 200°C. Place the tatin over a high heat on the stove and cook for 3 mins or until you see a bronze caramel appearing up the edges all the way round the tatin pan.

Place in the oven for 20 mins. Have a resting rack ready and once the time is up turn your tatin out onto the wire resting rack.

To finish Cut the tatin into quarters using a sharp knife and put a quarter on each plate. Serve with a scoop of vanilla ice cream and some of the warm caramel sauce.

< Apple tart tatin

05 **Crabshakk**
David Scott
Head chef

"If you're a lover of seafood Crabshakk is the place for you"

I first got involved in hospitality 24 years ago in the East Neuk of Fife where my father was a fisherman and my mother a cook. I tried my hand as a fisherman, but it didn't work for me, so I became a cook. I worked in a few local restaurants, and always had a passion for cooking seafood. I then spread my wings and moved to Glasgow and worked in a variety of restaurants before becoming head chef at a new seafood restaurant, the Crabshakk, opened by John MacLeod and Lynne Jones in the Finneston district of Glasgow. That was fifteen years ago, and I've been here since.

Since then, we've opened a new unit in the West End, Crabshakk Botanics, which is thriving. Both restaurants are doing well and have become established on the Glasgow culinary map.

If you're a lover of seafood Crabshakk is the place for you. On occasion I like to treat fish like meat. Roast it, rest it or serve it on the bone or off the bone. You can make great sauces from roasted fish bones. There's such a huge variety of fish that comes from these islands such as cuttlefish, seabream, blue fin tuna and so on that we're excited to promote and serve to customers.

There will be customers who might not like seafood but then we can do things at Crabshakk such as roast a John Dory on the bone just like a chicken, but it's still a John Dory, the same with turbot, halibut, and monkfish. There's such a variety of ways to prepare, cook and serve fish. And if fish is not to your taste, we've got crabcakes and shellfish such as delicious scallops with anchovy and sage butter. We've got vegan options and cater for all dietary requirements.

I've got a great, dynamic, multicultural team at Crabshakk and we're not afraid to utilise or delve into any culture, say – go Nordic, Asian, Mediterranean and more. We make our food exciting and encourage our customers to try something new.

Our site in Finneston is a smaller, more intimate venue catering for up to 40 covers. Crabshakk Botanics is a much larger site and while it's also a restaurant we cater for a wide range of people. So, there can be people wanting to come in for a three-course dinner, but also people that might just want fish and chips with a coffee or drink, or a snack with a cocktail.

There is a tradition in the West End of restaurants as the evening progresses evolving into bars, still serving food, but with good music and catering to a more clubbing, nighttime crowd. Crabshakk Botanics. continues that tradition and is a combination of a café, coffee bar, nightclub and restaurant.

At both venues, we want the customer to leave with a skip in their step and a good appreciation of our food.

I've worked in hospitality in Glasgow for a long time and the Glasgow public have become much more discriminating in what they want to eat. They don't want every venue serving the same stuff. They want fresh, seasonal food using smaller producers with a wide variety of different ingredients. That goes down well with the Glasgow public and that's what we give them at Crabshakk.

Crab cakes with lemon mayo

Ingredients

Crab cakes

White crab claw meat - 250g. Picked (check for shell)

Red chilli - 1 tsp. Very finely chopped

Shallot - 1 tsp. Very finely chopped

Parsley - 1 tsp. Very finely chopped

Panko breadcrumbs - 100g

Mayonnaise - 3 tbsp

Lemon - Juice of 1/2 a lemon

Lemon mayo

Sunflower oil - 250 – 300ml

Egg yolk - 1

Dijon mustard - 1 tsp

White wine vinegar - 1 tbsp

Lemon juice - 3 – 4 tbsp

Salt to taste

Method

A signature since day one, our Crab Cakes – we recommend making your own mayonnaise, but adding lots of lemon to your favourite shop bought brand will do nicely too.

For the crab cakes Mix everything together in a big bowl. Season with salt. Mould into 12 small patties. 30g each.

Make ahead and keep in the fridge until needed.

For the lemon mayo In a food processor or bowl with a whisk, add the egg yolk, mustard, vinegar and a pinch of salt. Blend or whisk until emulsified and then start to slowly pour in the oil in a steady slow stream so the oil has a chance to mix with the eggs to prevent it from splitting.

Once you are happy with consistency, add the lemon juice and carry on mixing until incorporated. Taste and add more salt and lemon juice if needed.

Will store air tight in the fridge for 5 – 7 days.

To serve Fry the Crab Cakes gently in a non-stick pan for 1 – 2 mins each side until golden.

Serve with a dollop of your lemony mayonnaise, and a leafy salad. Delicious.

< Crab cakes with lemon mayo

Page 58 Oysters with Vietnamese dressing

Whole John Dory, chicken butter, mushrooms and baby leeks

Ingredients

Chicken butter - make the day before

Chicken wings - 2kg

Onions - 2. Sliced

Carrots - 2. Peeled and sliced

Celery sticks - 2. Sliced

Garlic bulbs - 2. Halved

Rosemary - 10g

Thyme - 10g

Bay leaves - 2

Vegetable oil - 40ml

White wine - 200ml

Madeira - 200ml

Butter - 250g. Cold, cubed

Double cream - 150ml

Lemon juice - 2 tbsp

Salt to taste.

Mushroom - 200g. Chanterelles, oyster or maitake

Baby leeks/spring onions - 2 bunches

Herb oil

Chives - 50g. Halved

Tarragon - 50g. Leaves removed from stalk

Vegetable oil - 150ml

John Dory

John Dory - 4. 400 – 500g. Gutted and gills removed or ask your fishmonger to do this for you.

Method

This recipe is written for 4 individual John Dory, however if you can get one large John Dory around 1.5kg from your fishmonger it will make an outstanding centre piece.

Chicken butter sauce Roast chicken wings until golden brown. While wings are roasting slice the vegetables. Sauté the vegetables and garlic in some veg oil until starting to caramelise. Deglaze the pan with 200ml white wine and then add the wings herbs and then top up with water and slowly simmer for 3 – 4 hours. Topping up if needed.

Pass the stock into another pot and reduce to a jus. When a jus consistency has been reached, add 200ml Madeira and 150ml double cream and bring back to a boil and transfer to blender or use hand blender to emulsify the cold butter in to the sauce. Finish with lemon juice and salt to taste.

Mushrooms Brush clean and cut down to smaller bite size pieces and then sauté in hot pan with small amount of oil and salt until just cooked. Leave to cool on paper towel.

Leeks Blanch the leeks whole in salted water until just tender. Remove and refresh in cold water. Drain on paper towel once cold and when drained slice to similar size as mushrooms.

Herb oil Blanch leaves in salted boiling water for 15 secs. Refresh in iced water and then dry on paper towel or a cloth. Blitz the dried herbs with 150ml oil and a pinch of salt for 3 – 4 mins.

Pass through a fine sieve or paper towels.

John Dory Preheat your oven to 180°C. Once your dory is cleaned and your sauce, mushroom, leeks and herb oil are all ready its time to cook the fish.

Cook the fish in a non stick or heavy based pan with non stick paper down with salt and oil. 2 mins on both sides then move to the oven for 5 – 6 mins until the fish is just cooked.

For the larger fish, extend your time in the oven to 7 – 8 mins until the fish is just cooked.

While the fish is resting reheat your butter sauce with the mushrooms, leeks and chives.

To serve Divide the sauce between 4 plates and drizzle with herb oil and then place the john dory on top and enjoy.

< Whole John Dory, chicken butter, mushrooms and baby leeks

Page 59 Pistachio and lemon cake with fresh ricotta

Oysters and Vietnamese dressing

Ingredients

Oysters - 12. Shucked. We recommend using Loch Fyne

Spring onion - 1. Finely chopped

Red chilli - 1/2 tsp. Finely chopped

Ginger - 1 tsp. Grated

Garlic - 1/2 tsp. Grated

Tamari or light soy - 6 tbsp.

Rice wine vinegar - 4 tbsp

Lime juice - 2 tbsp

Fish sauce - 1 tbsp

Toasted sesame oil - 1 tbsp

Sugar - 1 tsp

Micro coriander or torn coriander leaf for garnish.

Method

You can make this in advance and will store in the fridge for 5 – 7 days. Mix all the ingredients together and check seasoning is correct.

To serve Spread ice or rock salt on your dish of choice, place the oysters on the ice or salt for stability then dress the oyster in the shell with the dressing and finish with a garnish of micro coriander or torn coriander leaf.

Pistachio and lemon cake with fresh ricotta

Ingredients

Cake

Lemons - 5
Ground pistachio - 200g
Ground almond - 100g
Golden caster sugar - 300g
Baking powder - 2 tsp
Eggs - 7

Ricotta

Full fat milk - 700 ml
Double cream - 240ml
Sea salt - 5g
Lemon juice - 30ml

Method

Cake Boil whole lemons until soft (1.5 hours). Allow to cool, cut in half and remove seeds.

Preheat oven to 160°C and line a 20cm cake tin with baking paper.

Blend lemons (including skin and pith) in a food processor, retain 450g and discard the rest.

Mix with dry ingredients. Add eggs 1 by 1 and mix until you have smooth batter. Pour mix into the prepared tin and bake for 45 mins – 1 hour. The cake will start to come away slightly from the sides of the tin.

Place on a wire rack and allow cake to cool in tin.

Ricotta Heat everything together on the stove top. Bring up to 70°C then take it off the heat. Cool at room temperature for 15 mins.

Place a muslin or clean tea cloth over a sieve and allow the liquid to strain through. The solids will remain in the cloth – this is your ricotta. Gently squeeze the ricotta to dry it.

Chill at least 1 hour before serving.

To Serve A perfect slice on a plate, with a good dollop of ricotta, grate some lemon zest over the top. Simple.

06 Celentanos
Dean Parker Head chef and co-owner

I was born in South Africa and moved to the UK after leaving school where I worked for a few mainly casual dining restaurants in London and discovered I had a passion for baking, which soon developed into cooking.

When I told my dad I wanted to be a chef he thought it was a "ridiculous suggestion" and I would only "last a year", so I was determined to prove him wrong. I moved on to work in higher end restaurants, ending up in the Royal Exchange under Robin Gill for ten years. Robin was an inspiration in how to motivate people to work together. Working with Robin, I was head chef at The Dairy, one of London's best neighbourhood restaurants. We developed something quite unique and, starting with a small budget we created something special. That's how I got started.

My wife, Anna, and I were keen to open our own restaurant before Covid and we viewed a few sites up in Glasgow. Then came lockdown and we had plenty of time to think about what we wanted to do. An opportunity came up at Cathedral House in Glasgow through someone Anna knew, and it felt like the right place at the right time. We named the restaurant after the Italian singer Adriano Celentano, who we heard a lot on our honeymoon around Italy.

Anna and I run the restaurant. Our food isn't what Scotland or Glasgow may know as "traditional" Italian, but we have taken a lot of inspiration from all different areas in Italy (there are so many different cooking styles), and the layout of our menu is traditional in Italy. We are nose to tail in our approach and make as much as we can ourselves, trying to be creative with our produce, even with the so called "waste products" where you can often get more from the byproduct than the prime cuts. We use local suppliers and produce, particularly a field to table farm outside Edinburgh called The Free Company.

Our approach to cuisine and dining is, it's not just about the food, but the experience. People come to a restaurant to eat, sure, but also to meet and celebrate. It's about the essence of hospitality which is missed a lot of the time.

Commitment and dedication are essential in running a restaurant. People often see running a restaurant as quite a romantic thing – preparing delicious food, serving happy, satisfied customers and so on – but it's the background things that can cause the most stress. Having to maintain equipment that's constantly breaking down is always hard. But you always appear in front of the customer with a smile on your face. You need to learn from the hardest mistakes – if you learn from them, you can eventually find positives in them and grow as a person or business.

I love Glasgow, the people are amazing, it's been a new lease of life and a whole new experience for me. Anna is from here and her whole family live nearby, it is so nice to have them around on our days off. It has taken us a long time to build a strong team at Celentano's, but we have a hard-working team now and feel very grateful for that. You need a good team around you in hospitality to make the long days enjoyable and we've got that.

"It's not just about the food, but the experience"

BBQ whole mackerel, rhubarb pickle, seaweed butter, ferikake

Ingredients

Whole mackerel

Fish - 4. 200 – 400g each

Water - 500ml

Salt - 40g

Sugar - 25g

Vegetable oil

Rhubarb pickle

Rhubarb - 2 sticks. Thinly sliced

White wine vinegar - 500ml

Water - 200ml

Sugar - 200g

Salt - 20g

Ferikake

Roasted sesame or sunflower seeds - 200g

Nori - 5 sheets

Green peppercorns - 20g

Dried shiso - 3g. Optional

Dark roasted kombu - 1 sheet

Dried lemon leaves - 10. Optional

Kombu salt - 20g. Or 10g rock salt

Seaweed butter

Butter - 500g

Fermented dulse - 50g. You can use dried dulse. If using dried – 3g

Toasted kombu - 50g

Sea nori sheets - 60g

Nocelara olives - 10. Pitted

Smoked paprika - 5g

Olive oil - 100ml

Salted capers - 20g

Lemon zest - 2 lemons

Garlic cloves - 3

Method

Serves 4

This is one of the easiest and tastiest fish to cook and prepare in my opinion. You can buy from a fish monger, and request them to scale and gut the fish.

Whole mackerel Make a brine by adding the water, salt and sugar together in a pot. Brine the fish by submerging it for approximately 10 mins and gently rub while in the brine. Remove and leave on a rack for 5 mins. If possible, hang in fridge overnight.

To BBQ, temper the fish by leaving out the fridge for approximately 20 mins before cooking. Ensure your coals are all red, and add a dampened piece of oak to the side of the coals if possible. Once there is a little smoke from the fire, rub the fish with a little vegetable oil. Start with the fish at a higher level on the BBQ so it starts to temper. Turn the fish after 3 mins.

Check the temperature of the fish (by using the probe at the centre). Once it is at approximately 30 – 25°C, lower the fish on the BBQ slightly. The fat will start to come off the fish, and you'll have some smoke from the heat. The flesh should start to golden – turn the fish over and ensure evenly golden on both sides. Check the temperature again. It should be 45°C (you don't want to go over 50°C). Remove from the heat.

Rhubarb pickle Place thinly sliced rhubarb in a pan, then pour over the remaining rhubarb pickle ingredients and bring to the boil. Leave this to cool. Tip – don't waste the juice. You can use this another time for salad dressings, or even in cocktails.

Ferikake Blend nori sheets until made into a fine dust. Add 1/2 the sesame seeds, and the rest of the ingredients and blend until a mixed powder is created. Add the other 1/2 of the sesame seeds and mix in a bowl.

Seaweed butter Sweat the garlic down with 500g butter until golden – then remove from the heat. Add the rest of the ingredients and fill the sink up with cold water. Place the pot in the cold water (ensure only about 1/2 up the outside of the pot) until tepid. Blend well and serve.

To serve Warm plates in the oven. Place fish at the side of the plate and brush the fish with the seaweed butter. Drain the pickled rhubarb and place 2 large tbsp of the rhubarb on top of the fish. We place the rhubarb on the fish to replicate scales. Dust the fish with ferikake for seasoning. Cut a wedge of lemon, and serve to the side of the fish. If you have dill available, pick dill fronds and sprinkle over the dish.

< BBQ whole mackerel, rhubarb pickle, seaweed butter, ferikake

Page 64/65 Agnolotti, sweetcorn, hazelnut ragu, girolles, toasted breadcrumbs. Agnolotti pasta

Agnolotti pasta

Serves 6 large portions or 12 small portions

Ingredients

Semolina flour - 500g
Pasta flour - 200g
Egg yolks - 100g
Whole eggs - 200g
EVOO - 6ml
Salt - 6g

Method

Add all liquids to mixing bowl and lightly mix. Add dry ingredients to the same bowl and mix well. Tip – add an extra yolk if it's crumbling. Mix dough until smooth and consistent. This should take between 3 – 4 mins.

Remove the dough from the bowl. Flatten it into 2 rectangles. Wrap it up in cling film pressing out the air as you wrap. Leave out of the fridge if rolling on the same day. If rolling next day, refrigerate and temper before rolling to soften dough.

Rolling the pasta – roll the dough down to 2mm to width of roller. It should be cut into 4 sections. Turn dough 90 degrees and roll again to 0.5mm. Repeat this one more time. Cut the pasta dough length ways into 6cm strips. Pipe the ricotta in cylinders from one side to the other, fold over and press the end to seal, by using 2 fingers on each press. Cut along the top with an agnolotti cutter.

Ensure you are allowing space for cutting when you seal each end. If you have any off-cuts, this can be saved and used for another pasta dish. Keep in fridge on an open tray allow 12 per person for large portion and 6 pieces for a small portion.

Agnolotti, sweetcorn, hazelnut ragu, girolles, toasted breadcrumbs

Ingredients

Corn Purée

Cooked corn - 150g. Remove kernels – see prep

Garlic - 20g. Finely sliced

Whey or vegetable stock - 300g

Organic soy miso or barley miso - 20g

Butter - 150g

Hazelnut Ragu

Hazelnuts - 300g

Butter - 250g

Shallots - 250g. Diced

Garlic - 20g. Chopped

Whey - 500ml

Organic soy miso - 20g

Lemon zest - 1 lemon

Toasted breadcrumbs

Dried sourdough bread - 100g. Blended into small crumbs

Olive oil - 30ml

Garlic - 1/2 clove

Bay leaf of thyme stalks

Cooked corn

Corn on cob - 1 large. With leaves on

Water

Salt

Girolles (for plating)

Mushrooms - 150g

Chives - 1 bunch

Plating

Corra Linn, or any hard cheese

Basil or marjoram

Method

Serves 4

This dish can be made with any pasta shape but is best made with freshly made agnolotti.

Corn purée Heat a large pot on medium heat with butter. Heat until the butter is lightly golden. Add garlic and lightly fry until golden then turn up the temperature. Add the corn and fry until lightly golden then turn the temperature down. Add the whey and bring to boil then cover. Don't let it reduce – cook for 5 mins. Place the mix in a blender and blend on high speed for about 3 – 5 mins then strain with a sieve into a heatproof container. Cover with cling film so that it doesn't skin. Leave out to cool.

Hazelnut Ragu Roast nuts until golden at around 175°C for roughly 10 mins. Leave to cool for 20 mins. Pulse the nuts in a food blender until they are roughly broken into quarters. Heat a medium pot and add butter. Bring to golden on a medium heat. Add garlic and fry until golden. Then add shallots. Once soft, (this will take about 5 mins) add the hazelnuts and cover with whey. Bring to the boil. Taste before adding miso – this is for seasoning, so season to your taste. Add the zest of one lemon.

Toasted breadcrumbs Add all ingredients to a roasting tray and give a good mix. Bake at 140°C for 15 – 20 mins. Remove garlic cloves and herbs before serving.

Cooked corn Fill 1 medium pot with water (large enough to fit the corn). Season the water lightly with salt to taste. Boil the water, add the corn and cook for 8 mins with lid on. Leave the corn to cool in pot with lid on once cooked. Remove leaves cut corn in half short ways then remove kernels from husk.

Girolles (for plating) Wash the mushrooms in a bath of water then drain and pat dry on cloth the day before you are cooking. Leave in the fridge in an open tray to dry. If large cut into 1/4 if small into 1/2. Separately slice 1/4 bunch of chives very fine and keep for finishing pasta.

To serve Boil agnolotti for 2 mins in seasoned water. In a flared saucepan, place puree in, then mix a little bit of whey emulsion if you have to lighten it up. Bring to simmer add girolles and cook gently for 1 min. Add corn kernels. In a separate pot, heat up the hazelnut ragu. Drain pasta, add to sauce pan with girolles, corn and chives. Gently fold pasta through. Plate agnolotti on heated plates, then sprinkle nut ragu over the pasta pieces. Crumble breadcrumbs over. Grate with Corra Linn cheese (or any hard cheese). Finish with fresh basil or marjoram.

Glazed rib on the bone with Jersey Royal salad

Ingredients

Whole rib of beef on the bone - You can buy one from your local butcher

Large onions - 10. Cut in half

Beef stock - 5l

Marmite - Optional. For seasoning

Method

Serves 8

We buy whole cows from local farm, preferably a smaller cow as they are less damaging on water logged fields and therefore more sustainable. We buy our meat and then age for at least 4 weeks. You can buy a whole rib on the bone from your local butcher. You can ask where they source this to ensure from a local farm.

Whole beef rib on the bone Temper the rib by keeping out of the fridge for at least 2 hours before cooking. Heat up a cast iron pan on the BBQ until base starts to smoke slightly. Place the rib in the pan, fat cap down and golden – gently turn the rib so the colour is even. Take off the heat, place on a tray and rub with salt and pepper.

Next – make sure the coals on your BBQ are all red (if you can, place a log just on the edge of the fire to catch the flames and create some wooded smoke). Start by placing the rib at about 35 – 40cm above the coals to temper gently, smoking on one side. Once you have it at 40°C (can check this with a temperature probe), turn your steak and lower it down to about 15cm above the red coals.

Once charring begins on the meat, check the temperature in the centre and on the meat next to the bone. You want this to be around 45°C. Turn steak and lower to 10cm above red coals until charring develops. Raise the steak back to 35cm above coals to reduce the speed of cooking – temp of meat should still be 48 – 50°C. Cook and smoke with the log until the meat reaches around 52°C.

Ensure to allow 15 mins resting time before serving. Suggest to serve with 150ml meat glaze (see below). Remove bone by cutting top end to bottom of the bone, remove base of bone by carving on an angle (stay close to the bone to reduce meat wastage). Carve the rib in 1cm slices, keeping the shape intact if possible. Season with rock salt, serve on a heated plate and spoon over glaze to your taste.

Meat glaze Boil onions in the stock. Place the onions in a large heavy pot and cover. Slowly cook on a very low heat for 6 – 8 hours. Once cooked, remove and strain the stock using a sieve into another pot. Place the liquid pot on high heat to reduce the liquid by half. Ensure it doesn't over boil. Separately, reduce 500ml Worcester sauce by placing on a high heat until it reduces to approx. 200ml. Add this to the reduced stock, then add 200ml malt extract. You can then season with marmite to taste.

To serve Serve with some Jersey Royal salad - recipe on the next page.

< Glazed rib on the bone with Jersey Royal salad

Page 69 Choux bun, miso cream, pickled wild berries, milk gelato

Jersey Royals, pea and mint salad

Ingredients

Pea salad

Podded peas - 1kg. Keep pea shells for puree later

Celery - 1 head. Dice 0.5 cm slices and season with 1% salt of their weight

Fresh mint - 1 bunch. Remove stalks and keep aside

Jersey Royals - 1kg

Wild garlic or chives - 100g

EVOO - 50ml

Pea purée

Frozen peas - 350g

Pea juice - 200ml. You can get this from juicing pea shells or use the blanching water from blanching your fresh peas with mint stalks in water

Olive oil - 50ml

Salt - 5g

Whey - 500ml

Organic soy miso - 20g

Lemon zest - 1 lemon

Method

Serves 4

Pea salad Put peas in a sieve and place the sieve in 1l seasoned salty water with half the mint stalks for 2 mins (keep the boiled water and pea shells for pea puree later). After the 2 mins of boiling, refresh for 2 mins (do this by removing the peas in a sieve, and placing the sieve in iced water for 2 mins). Chop wild garlic (or chives) very finely. Simmer potatoes in seasoned water for 20 mins with some of the rest of the mint stalks. Drain and leave to cool.

Tip – if you're doing this salad for a BBQ, grill the potatoes on a BBQ after cooking. Simply rub with EVOO, some salt and char over a hot BBQ until the skins start to blister turn over, repeat. Remove from grill leave to cool.

Cut potatoes in half and dress with a generous serving of EVOO and mix with chives. Chop the celery finely into the 0.5cm dices and season. Leave aside for building the plate later.

Pea purée Use the water from your fresh peas of the salad to boil the frozen peas. Boil the peas for 1 min, drain then add to blender. Add the pea juice and 5g salt. Blend until smooth. Pass over ice water by placing 300ml water and 200g ice into a bowl, then place an empty bowl on top. Strain the purée into the top bowl using a fine sieve. Leave aside for plating.

To finish Add purée to base of plate or bowl. Evenly place potatoes on top of purée. Mix the peas with the diced celery then place over potatoes. Tear fresh mint leaves over peas and celery. And serve.

Choux bun, miso cream, pickled wild berries, milk gelato

Ingredients

Choux crackling

Butter - 250g
Demerara sugar - 250g
Rye flour - 250g
Salt - 250g

Choux bun

Butter - 250g
Whole milk - 250ml
Strong bread flour - 250g
Water - 250ml
Salt - 10g
Sugar - 25g
Whole eggs - 7
Bay leaf - 1

Miso cream

Whole milk - 200ml
White chocolate - 130g
Cheese rind - 30g
Gelatine - 2 sheets
Mascarpone - 300g
Miso - 18g

Pickled berries and currant gel

Blackberries - 1 punnet
Blackcurrants - 1 punnet
Gooseberries - 1 punnet
Water - 300ml
Sugar - 300g
White wine vinegar - 300ml
Agar agar - 300g
Virgin olive oil - 25ml

Milk gelato

Milk - 1l
Glucose - 50g
Whipping cream - 280g
Milk powder - 200g
Sugar - 185g
Salt - 9g
Gelatine - 1.5 sheets

Plating ingredients

Mint
Lemon balm of verbena

Method

Serves 4

Choux crackling In a large mixing bowl, add all the ingredients and mix well until you reach a dough consistency. Roll out into sheets, between baking parchment as thin as you can get it. Chill, then cut with a round.

Choux bun Boil liquids with the bay leaf, sugar, salt and butter. Remove the bay leaf then add the flour while whisking. Bring to 85°C. Remove all from the pan, and chill to 56°C. Place the dough in a mixer and add 1 egg at a time while beating. It should become a smooth silky consistency. Place the mixture into piping bags and seal. Tie the end. Leave to rest and chill for 20 mins before baking.

Pipe mixture onto baking paper at a weight of 20g. Place the disc of crackling on top of each piped dough, and bake immediately. Bake at 180°C. Remember to pre heat oven for 10 mins before baking. These can be pre baked a few hours before serving, but should only be baked on same day as serving as they will lose their crisp texture.

Miso cream Boil the milk with cheese rind and cover. Leave to infuse for 30 mins. Soak the gelatine leaves in cold water to soften, then re boil the milk and cheese – add the gelatine and whisk. In a bowl, weight up the white chocolate and miso. Strain the milk gelatine mix over the chocolate. Leave for 5 mins then whisk gently until it melts completely. Once melted, add the mascarpone and chill. Once cold, you can whisk until fluffy and place in a piping bag. Store in fridge until ready to use.

Pickled berries and currant gel Pick stems off berries and keep each berry type in separate sealed containers. Boil the water, sugar and vinegar then pour over the berries (still in separate containers) to pickle. Leave to cool. Take 300ml for the blackcurrants, add 300g agar and then bring to the boil and leave to simmer for 5 mins. Leave to cool – this should set into a gel. Blend this gel until smooth with 25ml virgin olive oil and place in a squeezy bottle in fridge until you need it.

Milk gelato Bring the rest of the ingredients to the boil in a pot, then add the gelatine. Leave to cool then churn in an ice cream maker. Ideally churn 2 hours before serving. Set in freezer.

To serve Place plates in freezer 1 hour prior to serving. Make small holes in the bottom on the choux buns, and fill them with the miso cream. Place buns off centre on your plate. Drain the berries and gently mix them all together. Spread about a table spoon of gel next to the choux, leaving a small gap for the gelato, place berries onto gel. Spoon a roche of gelato between the berries and choux. Garnish the berries with your herb of choice.

07 The East End Fox
Ferrier Richardson
Chef proprietor

"Using the best ingredients available daily, keeping it simple and using modern techniques and skills."

When I started college, it was always my plan to go into hotel management, but during my management course I realised I enjoyed the cooking side of things much more and started my career at the Central Hotel in Glasgow as a Commis Chef.

Many years on, I am now the chef/proprietor of The East End Fox, a gastro pub in the East End of Glasgow. When we opened, many people were 'surprised' at the location and the style of venue as previously I'd only been associated with running award winning stylish high-end restaurants, five-star Hotels, and looking after wealthy clients and heads of state, in various parts of the world, which I still do, when requested.

Returning to Glasgow after twenty years away, I realised that the quality mid-market sector was where most dinners were gravitating towards, and my vision was to provide customers of The East End Fox with great "Elevated Comfort Food".

It's worked out well. The East End Fox has won the Drams and Greene Kings' Pub of the Year awards and is among the final five contestants for the British Pub of the Year award 2024. Business is good, though you must work at it every day, to re-energise and enthuse your customer base and your staff.

I would describe my 'food philosophy' as using the best ingredients available daily, keeping it simple and using modern skills and techniques. For example, with our Friday night Chateaubriand Steak board or our Sunday roast, we will water bath these dishes for the required period, then finish them in the oven, before serving, to give them a delicious flavour and tenderness.

There have been many challenging events in my culinary career but one that really stands out was when I was Executive Private Chef to the President of Gabon in Central Africa. On the anniversary of the President's father's death, I prepared food for an event to commemorate the anniversary and placed the dishes in large cool boxes before flying in a Chinook helicopter to the presidential palace.

After the helicopter landed, I took the cool boxes off and set them down a distance away before standing back to gaze at the awesome sight of the Chinook taking off again. The only thing was that every bloody cool box went flying along the ground or into the air as the chopper left the beautiful Palace grounds.

Luckily, the food stayed in the boxes. Later, after the dinner, the President and I had a good laugh about "the flying cool box incident".

The East End Fox, has been a great success with the local community. I recall when we first opened a woman posted on Facebook "who do these people think they are, charging these prices in the east end of Glasgow?" Before I could respond, there was an avalanche of local people attacking her saying "are we not good enough for quality food, wine and a stylish venue such as this?"

The woman who posted the comment, came in personally to see me two days later and apologised, which I accepted, and she's now been won over. I was so pleased with our customer's responses. It showed they had bought into my vision and has certainly made me realise how lucky we are, to have a clientele who appreciate all our hard work and endeavours, as we do them; long may it continue.

Peking duck spring rolls, hoisin dipping sauce

Ingredients

Hoisin sauce - 300ml
Half Peking duck (Chung Ying)
Vegetable oil - 4 tbsp
Sesame oil - 2 tbsp
Red pepper - 1/2 medium. Sliced into matchstick thin strips
Green pepper - 1/2 medium. Sliced into thin matchstick strips
Yellow pepper - 1/2 medium. Sliced into thin matchstick strips
Carrot - 1 medium. Peeled and sliced into thin matchstick strips
White onion - 1 medium. Peeled, halved and sliced thinly. Separate leaves
Garlic - 1 tsp. Finely chopped
Ginger - 1 tsp. Finely chopped
Red chilli - 1 tsp. Finely chopped
Fresh coriander - 2 tbsp. Chopped
1 egg - Plus 100 ml water for egg wash
Medium spring roll wrappers - 16

Method

Serves 4

Add vegetable and sesame oils to a frying pan or wok, warm.

Add peppers, carrot, onion, garlic, ginger and chilli and stir-fry. Keep a light bite to the vegetables, decant onto a tray and allow to cool.

Cook Peking duck as per instructions on packet. When warm to touch, remove bones, shred and chill.

Mix vegetables, chopped fresh coriander, chilled shredded duck and 4 tbsp of hoisin sauce. Divide the mixture into 16 portions.

Place one wrapper like a diamond, pastry brush the edges of wrapper with egg wash and fill bottom section of wrapper with one portion of the mix in the bottom corner of the spring roll.

Roll into a sealed cylinder and seal with egg wash (If you look on You Tube, you will find a video on how to roll the perfect spring roll).

When all spring rolls are ready, deep fry at 180°C for 6 mins until golden brown. Cook in batches that suit the size of your deep fat fryer. Do not overload the fryer. If frying in batches have your oven at 100°C to keep the first batch warm.

Line a bamboo basket with a bamboo leaf, or grease proof paper. Add a small ramequin dish with two tablespoons of hoisin sauce and, if you like a touch of mixed salad or Asian noodle salad and add your tasty spring rolls.

Bamboo baskets, hoisin sauce, spring roll wrappers and Peking Duck can all be bought at Chung Ying Supermarket, 254 Dobbies Loan, Glasgow. It's been my go to Chinese supermarket for over 30 years. Bamboo leaves on Amazon Prime.

< Peking duck spring rolls, hoisin dipping sauce

Page 76 Roast chateaubriand with fries, mac and cheese, onion rings, roast tomatoes...

Roast scallops, butternut squash purée, black pudding bon bons, curry and coriander oil

Ingredients

Scallops

Scottish scallops - 12 Large. Roe removed

Olive oil - 3 tbsp

Sea Salt and white pepper

Lemon - 1/2

Unsalted butter - 1 tbsp

Black pudding bon bons

Black pudding - 240g. Divided into 8 pieces

Plain flour - 100g

Eggs - 2. Whisked into 200ml of milk

Panko breadcrumbs - 150g

Squash puree

Butternut squash - 250g. Peeled and deseeded

Unsalted butter - 100g

Garlic - 1 tbsp. Chopped

Ginger - 1 tbsp. Chopped

Onion - 1/2 medium. Finely chopped

Vegetable stock - 100ml

Curry oil

Rapeseed oil - 100ml

Hot Madras curry powder - 1 tbsp

Cumin seeds - 1/2 tsp

Coriander seeds - 1/2 tsp

Turmeric - 1/2 tsp

Corriander oil

Rapeseed oil - 100ml

Baby spinach - 200g

Coriander - 30g

Garnish

Pea shoots - 1 pkt

Method

Curry oil Temper the dry spices in a dry medium-hot pan for thirty secs. Cover with 200ml oil, warm the seasoned oil, then cool, pass through a fine sieve, place in a small squeezy bottle.

Coriander oil Bring a large pan of salted water to a boil, blanche the spinach and coriander for 10 secs remove and place immediately into iced water.

Drain the coriander and spinach, squeeze dry in a clean tea towel, blitz in a food mixer with 250ml rapeseed oil, season, then pass through a fine sieve. Place in a small squeezy bottle.

Squash puree In a medium pan add butter, sweat the onion, garlic, seasoning and ginger till soft, add the diced squash, add vegetable stock and cook gently until soft, remove from the pan and blitz in a blender until super smooth. Keep warm.

Black pudding bon bons Roll the black pudding into 8 balls, roll them in seasoned flour, then egg wash. Next coat the balls with the panko crumbs. Place on a tray. Deep fry at 180°C for 4 mins to achieve a light golden colour. Keep warm.

Scallops Season the scallops with olive oil, sea salt and white pepper. Sear over medium to high heat for 1 min – golden brown colour, finish with a squeeze of lemon and a tbsp of butter.
Tip – place the scallops in the pan clockwise so you know which ones went in first.

Plating We use an oblong plate. Place a good tbsp of the squash puree on each plate on the left hand side, then gently smear across the plate, alternate scallop, bon bon, scallop, bon bon, scallop, dress with the two flavoured oils and some pea shoots.

For two years I worked with the leading Professor in the world for osteoporosis in Surrey developing algorithms. This is a dish I served him, so I know all the ingredients can be bought in Waitrose. Not the cheapest, but a great store for quality ingredients.

< Roast scallops, butternut squash purée, black pudding bon bons, curry and coriander oil

Roast Chateaubriand with fries, mac and cheese, onion rings, roast tomatoes and mushrooms and a brandy peppercorn sauce

Ingredients

Roast Chateaubriand

Head of Scottish beef fillet - 1kg. trimmed and rolled

Sea salt, ground black pepper

Unsalted butter - 2 tbsp

Olive oil - 2 tbsp

Pea shoots - 1 Pkt. Or 1 bunch of watercress

Onion rings

Rice flour - 25g

Corn flour - 25g

Self-rising flour - 100g

Onion - 1. Large

Soda water - 1/2 pint. Very cold

Roast mushrooms and tomatoes

Plum tomatoes - 2

Field mushroom - 4

Olive oil - 4 tbsp

Dried Provencal herbs - 1 tsp

Garlic - 1 tsp. Finely Chopped

Mac and cheese

Plain flour - 100g

Unsalted butter - 100g

Milk - 500ml

Salt and white pepper

Strong cheddar - 200g. Grated

English mustard powder - 1 tsp.

Worcestershire sauce - 2 tbsp

Macaroni - 200g

Parmesan - 100g. Grated

Peppercorn sauce

Unsalted butter - 1 tbsp

Onion - 1 tbsp. Finely chopped

Crushed black peppercorns - 2 tbsp

Cooking brandy - 50ml

Red wine - 100ml

Beef or veal stock - 200ml

Double cream - 100ml

Chives - 1 tbsp. Finely chopped

Method

Serves 4

Roast Chateaubriand Remove the meat from the fridge and allow to come to room temperature. Season with salt and black pepper.

Seal the meat on all sides in a medium to hot pan with olive oil and butter, place meat in a convection oven 180°C until it reaches an internal temperature of preferably 54°C, baste continuously whilst cooking.

54°C for medium rare, 58°C for medium. Remove from the oven cover lightly with foil and rest for 15 mins.

Cut into 12 even slices onto a nice wooden platter or warm serving plate, garnish with Pea shoots or Watercress.

Onion rings Cut onion into rings. Add all dry ingredients into a bowl and mix thoroughly, season, add soda water to make the batter. Dip the rings into the batter and fry at 185°C until crispy and golden, drain onto kitchen paper. Then place in a warm serving dish.

Roast mushroom and roast tomatoes Remove the calyx from the tomato and cut length ways. Gently coat with olive oil, season with sea salt, black ground pepper, Provencal herbs and garlic.

Remove the stock and peel the mushroom, season with salt, black ground pepper and olive oil. Place the tomato and mushroom into a 200°C convection oven for 10 mins.

Mac and cheese Add the pasta and boil until al dente. Drain, refresh. To make the cheese sauce, melt the butter over medium heat add the flour and stir until smooth. Add the milk slowly until all is incorporated and the sauce is smooth, cook on a medium heat for a further 5 mins.

Stir in the Cheddar cheese, English mustard powder, Worcestershire sauce, add to macaroni, until you have a nice ratio of pasta to sauce, place into a gratin dish, dust with grated parmesan on top and glaze.

Peppercorn sauce Melt butter in a medium saucepan. Add chopped onions gently cook but do not colour, add crushed peppercorns, brandy and red wine. Then reduce by 1/2, add stock, reduce by 2/3, then add cream and cook until the sauce coats the back of a spoon. Finish with chopped chives.

French Fries 500g of fine cut chips blanched in oil at 140°C until al dente, then finish at 190°C until golden brown. Or alternatively cook quality frozen fries as per instruction on the packet. Season with sea salt.

This is a multi-task recipe but well worth the effort, a bit of a showstopper when brought to the table. If you have two ovens keep one at 100°C to keep food warm as it is ready.

Sticky toffee pudding souffle

Ingredients

Sticky toffee pudding

Soft pitted dates - 115g. Roughly chopped

Boiling water - 140ml

Bicarbonate of soda - 1/2 tsp

Unsalted butter - 45g. Plus extra for greasing

Caster sugar - 45g

Dark muscovado sugar - 45g

Egg - 1 large

Self-raising flour - 100g. Plus extra for dusting

Toffee sauce

Caster sugar - 100g

Double cream - 100ml

Unsalted butter - 50g

Vanilla extract - 1/2 tsp

Souffle base

Milk - 250ml

Cornflour - 25g

Sticky toffee pudding - 50g. Pudding blitzed to a crumb

Caster Sugar - 50g

Rising ingredients

Egg whites - 200g

Caster sugar - 140g

To serve

Quality Vanilla Ice Cream - 4 balls

Method

Serves 4

Sticky toffee pudding

Step 1 - Tip the dates into a heatproof bowl and pour over the boiling water. Add the bicarbonate of soda, then leave the dates to soften and cool for 15 mins. Transfer the dates and their soaking water to the bowl of a small processor and blitz them to a smooth purée.

Step 2 - Cream the butter and both sugars together in the bowl of a mixer fitted with a beater attachment, on medium-high speed, for 3 – 5 mins, until light and fluffy. Add the egg and beat until combined. Add the flour and mix for about 1 min on low speed until combined, then add the puréed dates and fold them through the mixture, using a spoon or spatula, until no streaks remain and taking care not to over-mix.

Step 3 - Pour the cake batter into a suitable baking tin, cook at 160°C in a convection oven until pudding is springy to the touch and a skewer comes out clean. Cool.

Toffee sauce Tip the caster sugar into a small to medium saucepan and add 2 tbsp of water. Set the pan over a low heat to dissolve the sugar – don't stir, but gently swirl the pan from time to time. When the sugar has dissolved, increase the heat to medium and bring the syrup to the boil. Continue to cook until the syrup becomes a deep amber colour, swirling the pan gently to ensure that the caramel cooks evenly.

Remove the pan from the heat and carefully (as it will spit and splutter) add the cream and butter and stir gently to combine. Return the pan to a low heat to re-melt any hardened caramel. Add the vanilla and mix to combine. Remove the pan from the heat and leave the caramel sauce to cool to room temperature while you make the souffles.

Souffle Preheat convection oven to 185°C. Grease 4 medium ramekins with butter. Pour milk into a medium saucepan, and whisk in cornflour till dissolved. Mix in sugar and sticky toffee pudding crumb, place over medium heat bring to a boil, and simmer until thick. Remove from pan into a suitable container and chill.

Whisk egg whites until frothy in a pristine stainless-steel bowl, add sugar bit by bit until soft peaks emerge. Whisk 25% of egg mix into 300g of souffle base, then fold the rest in gently and divide between the four ramekins. Smooth the tops of the ramekins and cook in the middle of the oven in a water bath for 12 mins. Once sufficiently risen remove carefully and dust with icing sugar.

To serve Serve with a ball of quality vanilla ice cream and a bowl of toffee sauce.

08 Eusebi Deli

Giovanna Eusebi
Owner

My grandparents lived a simple sustainable life in Southern Italy. All the food they grew was organic and grown biodynamically. This sustainable way of living has left an indelible mark on me and defines all we do today. My father opened a greengrocer in the east end of Glasgow, in the early 70's, where he was born. It stocked simple Italian staples like olive oil, pasta, tomatoes before supermarkets made their mark on the retail landscape. It grew over the years, serving fresh, wholesome Italian food made from scratch. It was real food for real people. I began working in that shop from an early age and eventually worked full time there.

Many years later, my brother found a site in the West End of Glasgow, and we decided we'd open a restaurant alongside the deli. It's been a great success since, and become a fixture on the West End dining scene.

Eusebi is about celebrating the ethos as well as the diversity of the Italian food landscape. I mean by that the huge variety of its produce, its seasonality as well as all the regional variations. We make everything from scratch including fresh pasta, Roman sourdough pizza, breads & dolci from our bakery which sits on the original site of my parents' little shop.

It all goes back to my grandmother's house in Italy where her food was genuine, simple, free of pesticides. Her food, grown and made with love, is what everyone should be eating now. When we opened Eusebi, I wanted their food love journey to live on. I adapted all her simple ways of fresh seasonal cooking and share that old love with a new generation of chefs and customers.

One means of doing that is to celebrate Italian food and culture. We invite chefs, growers, makers, writers and so on to come in and narrate their story and talk about Italian culture through their eyes. But it always goes back to the basics which is serving good food, hard work and consistency. It's also vital that you care who you are cooking for. If someone asks me: 'how do you make good Italian food?' I would answer: 'with simple ingredients and a whole lot of sentiment.'

If you ask what my philosophy of food is at Eusebi is it's probably best summed up in the phrase: My truth, my table, my food. Or another way of putting it: Born in Italy, made in Glasgow.

Opening Eusebi in the West End was difficult; we had some hurdles and red tape which we've mainly overcome. We want to cultivate a European outlook with tables outside and promote an authentic Italian dining culture in this great city.

Then, of course, there was Covid, which were two very challenging years when you often didn't know from one week to the other what the rules were. We adapted by retaining our bakery at the east end deli because that allowed us to serve cakes as part of our takeaway offer which helped to keep us going. But we've came through all that bigger and better.

For me Eusebi, and hospitality in its entirety, is about people coming in as customers and leaving as friends. It's about humanity at it's kindest. You're not just serving food, important though that is, you're also creating a beautiful experience. It's truly vocational. I love seeing the reaction of people to their food, watching their body language; that is very fulfilling.

People make Eusebi, the buzzing, exciting place it is in the heart of the wonderful city of Glasgow. Come in and savour it.

"Born in Italy, made in Glasgow"

Pictured with Giovanna Eusebi – Head Chef Sebastian Wereski

Homemade ricotta with honey and crushed hazelnuts

Ingredients

Full cream organic milk - 750ml
Double cream - 250ml
Salt - 1/4 tsp
Lemon juice or white vinegar - 60ml

Garnish

Rosemary - 1 tsp. Finely chopped
Local honey - 1 tsp
Hazelnuts - 1 tsp. Toasted, chopped
Toasted ciabatta or focaccia - Thinly sliced
Season to taste

Making ricotta is easy. It's a dish which sits on every Spring menu and over the years has been modernised by our head chef Sebastian. This version is from our Spring menu 2018. The premise of making ricotta is inspired by my Nonna Maria's table in Southern Italy. Spring was heralded with new milk and celebrated like the arrival of a new born baby with homemade ricotta, fava beans and wild asparagus picked by my Grandfather.

Scottish milk is perfect. Use organic, full cream milk for best results.

Method

Serves 4

Make the ricotta In a heavy bottom pot gently heat up the liquid and salt until it reaches a temperature of 85°C.

Once the temperature has been reached add in the lemon juice or vinegar and gently stir twice to evenly distribute the acid. The mixture will curdle immediately.

Leave to settle untouched for 20 mins so the curds can form and rise to the surface.

With a slotted spoon transfer the curds into 4 ricotta moulds evenly and leave to set in the fridge for a few hours or overnight. If you don't have ricotta moulds, line a sieve with muslin.

To serve Tip the ricotta onto a plate and serve with a good local honey drizzled on top, with crushed toasted hazelnuts, chopped fresh rosemary, flaky salt, cracked black pepper and toasted focaccia.

< Homemade ricotta with honey and crushed hazelnuts

Page 84 Osso bucco

Crab ravioli

Ingredients

Pasta dough

'00' flour - 200g
Free range eggs - 2 large
Egg yolks - 2
Olive oil - 15ml

Crab filling

Crab meat - 100g. 50/50 white/brown meat
Mascarpone - 50g
Ricotta - 50g
Melted butter - 25g
Lemon - 1. Zest and juice
Parsley - 1 tbsp. Chopped
Chilli flakes - Pinch
Salt /pepper to taste

Butter sauce

Butter - 60g
Samphire - 40g
Tarragon - 1 tbsp. Chopped
Cherry tomatoes - 200g. Halved

In our original deli in the East End of Glasgow, we hand-rolled pasta every single day. A group of women ranging in ages from 30 – 90, united around a table kneading, stretching and chattering over the dull sound of the cranking Imperia pasta machine. We made the pasta the same way every day, as my grandmothers and their grandmothers did. There is a simple beauty in the bond of friendship that unites us through cooking together. When we opened the West End restaurant, fresh pasta was at the top of the page. The crab ravioli has been on our menu for many years. Sebastian has merged the very best of Scotland's larder with locally sourced crab meat and Nonna's pasta making. It's a labour of love but so worth it.

Method

Serves 4

Make the dough Make the flour into a well and add the eggs. Use a fork to incorporate a little of the flour with the egg, gradually scraping the flour from the sides of the bowl. If the dough is too dry add a little of the oil and gradually work it in. The consistency should start forming a messy ball.

Tip it out onto a floured surface. With both hands knead the dough folding it over itself away from you. Continue for 3 mins and rotate the dough by a quarter turn – repeating. Continue kneading until it's smooth. Wrap it in cling film and rest for 15 mins at room temperature. It can be refrigerated overnight wrapped in cling film. When ready to use, bring it out 15 mins before to allow it to get to room temperature.

Make the filling Put all the ingredients into a bowl and mix with a fork. Season to taste and set aside in the fridge.

Make the ravioli Flour your work surface lightly. Split the dough in half. Keep the piece you are not using covered with cling film or a damp tea towel to stop it drying out. Roll out your dough to a 2.5cm rectangular thickness. Put it through the widest setting of your pasta machine. Fold over and pass it through again dusting lightly with flour. Repeat gradually going down the settings to the second last thickness on your machine. Repeat with the other piece. Keep the pasta sheet (you are not using immediately), covered with cling film to avoid it drying out.

The sheet of dough should be silky. Lay the sheet horizontally on a floured work surface. With a teaspoon place the filling on one half of the rectangular length nearest you leaving a space of 1cm between the spooned fillings. Spray the sides of the exposed dough lightly with water. Flip the pasta sheet towards you like folding paper in half to cover the crab filling. Then seal along all the edges with the palm of your hand. Make sure to expel any air. Using a ravioli cutter run it along the longest horizontal edge in one run. Then cut along vertically to create your parcels. Place onto floured trays and set aside. Refrigerate if not using immediately.

To cook the ravioli and sauce. Bring a pan of water in a large pot to the boil. Season with salt to taste. Cook for 8 mins approx until the edges of the ravioli are soft but don't overcook.

Whilst the ravioli are cooking, make the sauce. Take a large pan and gently heat the butter until foaming. Add the cherry tomatoes and press with the back of a spoon. After a few mins add a little ladleful of the pasta water and reduce slightly. Add the herbs, samphire and drained ravioli.

Serve and season to taste if required.

< Crab ravioli

Page 85 Rum baba with orange mascarpone cream

Osso bucco

Ingredients

Osso bucco veal cutlets - 4. Dusted in flour

Olive oil - 2 tbsp

Butter - 50g

Onion - 1. Finely chopped

Carrot - 1. Finely chopped

Celery stick - 1. Finely chopped

Garlic - 1 head. Cut horizontally

Lemon - 2 strips of zest

Sage leaves - 8

White wine - 200ml

Chicken stock - 300ml

For the gremolata

Lemon - 1. Unwaxed. Zest finely grated

Garlic clove - 1. Very finely chopped

Flat-leaf parsley - 3 tbsp. Finely chopped

Sea salt - Pinch

Extra virgin olive oil - 50ml

For the risotto

Carnaroli risotto rice - 300g

Butter - 80g

Medium onion - 1. Finely chopped

White wine - 200ml

Hot chicken stock - 1.2l

Parmesan - 100g. Grated

Saffron - Generous pinch

Method

Serves 4

For the osso bucco Set a casserole dish wide enough to hold the meat in one layer over a high heat, and add the oil. When the oil is hot, add the meat to the pan and brown well on both sides until golden and crusted. Set aside on a plate.

Turn the heat down and add the butter to the pan. When melted, add the onion, carrot and celery, plus a sprinkle of salt, and cook until soft. Add the garlic halves, lemon zest and sage to the pan and cook for a few mins more.

Turn up the heat then add the wine to the pan. Return the meat, standing it on top of the vegetables, and bubble until the wine has reduced by half. Pour in the stock and bring to a simmer.

Turn the heat right down, cover and simmer for 1.5 – 2 hours, carefully turning the meat over every 30 mins, until it is tender enough to cut with a spoon.

Meanwhile, mix together the gremolata ingredients.

Heat half the butter with the olive oil in a saucepan, add the onion and cook for a few mins until beginning to soften. Stir in the saffron and cook for 1 min. Tip in the rice, mix well with the onion, and cook for 2 mins. Turn up the heat, pour in the wine and allow to bubble rapidly until it has been absorbed – about 2 mins.

Pre-heat the stock in a separate saucepan and gradually add to the rice, a ladleful at a time, allowing each ladleful to be absorbed before adding the next. Keep doing this, stirring frequently, until all the liquid has been added and absorbed by the rice, giving a creamy texture, this will take 16 – 18 mins.

Stir through the Parmesan and remaining butter. Season well to taste and allow to sit, covered, for a few mins.

To serve Divide the risotto between four plates. Top with the veal and spoon over the jus from the pan. Finish with a sprinkle of the gremolata.

Rum baba with orange mascarpone cream

Ingredients

For the baba

Strong flour - 125g

Salt - 1g

Sugar - 13g

Fresh yeast - 5g. Or active dry yeast - 2g

Egg - 125g

Butter - 45g. At room temperature

Syrup to soak the baba

Water - 225g

Rum - 100g

Caster sugar - 200g

Cinnamon stick - 1/2

Orange peel - 1/2 orange

Lemon peel - 1/2 lemon

Vanilla pod - 1/2

Star anise - 1/2

Orange mascarpone cream

Cream - 100g

Icing sugar - 50g

Babà was brought to Southern Italy in the nineteenth century by chefs who had trained in France and worked for the French aristocracy. The dessert became a local speciality of Naples and will grace the tables across Italy at all times of the year.

This is my mothers most favourite dessert. Darnell our head pastry chef has created this version to make at home, so easy to make and authentic.

Method

For the baba Combine the yeast, milk and 15g of flour to form a smooth ball of dough. Set in a bowl wrapped with cling film and leave to rise in a warm place for about 30 mins, or until doubled in size.

Place the remaining flour in a stand mixer with the paddle attachment. Add the yeast mixture and run on a medium-low speed. Add the sugar and eggs and let the mixer run for about 20 mins, until the dough becomes elastic and starts to come away from the side of the bowl.

Using the dough hook attachment, turn the mixer back on at a low speed and add the salt. Add the butter, one cube at a time, ensuring each cube is fully incorporated before adding the next one. After you add all the butter, keep working the dough for 10 more mins, until the dough looks soft and shiny.

Turn off the mixer, remove the bowl and wrap it in cling film. Leave the dough to rise in a warm place for 3 hours.

Once dough is ready, divide into balls of 50g each. Place the dough into small greased moulds which are approx 7cm in diameter and 7cm deep. You can get baba moulds, but easily use a savarin, dariole or a silicone donut mould. Cover with greased cling film and allow the dough to rise for another 1 – 2 hours until you can see the dough has risen and doubled in size again.

Place the babas into a preheated oven at 180°C for 12 mins. Remove the babas from the moulds and place on a baking tray. Bake for another 10 mins at 100°C. I like to leave them in the oven while switched off with the door slightly open to further remove any remaining moisture inside the baba. The baba should be dry like bread and firm.

To make the syrup Place the water in a pot and add the lemon peel, orange peel, vanilla, cinnamon, star anise, and sugar. Place the pot over a medium heat and bring to a simmer. Once the sugar has dissolved, remove the pot from the heat, allow it to cool slightly, then add the rum.

Once cooled the baba can be added to the syrup. These will keep for 1 week in an airtight container.

Best served warm or at room temperature.

Orange mascarpone cream Whip all together by hand or use a mixer until you get a smooth creamy consistency. This mix will keep 2 – 3 days in a refrigerator.

To serve Split the baba length ways. Pipe or spoon in the orange cream to fill the cavity. Drizzle some syrup around the Baba. You can garnish with orange peel or seasonal berries.

09 **Crossbasket Castle Hotel**

Kevin Barron
Executive chef

"Surrounded by beautiful, verdant grounds with a magical dining room set in a castle, our guests are swept up in the ambience of luxury and tranquillity."

My first step into the culinary world was when I was 14. I was visiting my aunt in Clydebank, who worked in a local hotel. I was looking for some work experience, and she was able to secure me a role in the kitchen. It ignited a passion in me for cooking, and the rest is history.

My career has taken me to wonderful places. One of the most memorable was a twelve-year stint in Kenya, where the produce was almost (I emphasise almost!) as good as Scotland, with beautiful fresh fish served just hours after being caught.

Today, I'm the executive chef at the magnificent Crossbasket Castle, near Glasgow. Not many people can say that they work in a 17th century historic Scottish castle – it's an incredible 'office'. Surrounded by beautiful, verdant grounds with a magical dining room set in a castle, our guests are swept up in the ambience of luxury and tranquillity. We are one of only ten hotels in Scotland to have received Five Red Stars, a kite mark and guarantee of quality.

The castle's 3 AA Rosette restaurant is overseen by the internationally acclaimed Chef Michel Roux Jnr. I work closely with him to devise dishes that will surprise, delight and showcase the best of what Scotland has to offer, with hints of French flair. We're steadfast in our commitment to Scottish produce, sourced locally – even the tomatoes are grown down the road.

Styles of cuisine and dining are constantly evolving. However, our ethos remains the same. Source, prepare and serve guests first class produce that follows the seasons. I like a twist, and I'm really excited about 'theatre' in dining over the last few years, which brings a new, multisensory dimension to the experience.

Working in a busy kitchen with extremely high standards isn't always easy, but if the kitchen is controlled and ready to go, we can rise to any test. Just recently, we provided a very successful five-star barbecue in the grounds for 50 guests. Being Scotland, it was pouring rain - but cancellation was not an option. Thanks to quick thinking from my fantastic team, we secured a gazebo and went on to serve up an epic feast, including pan fried scallops, rib of beef in black treacle and luxury hotdogs and burgers. It was a great success as the whole team pulled together.

I've mentioned it already, but the secret to a great kitchen really is the team: it is everything. Look after them and the rest will follow. I operate best in a relaxed yet disciplined kitchen and like to lead with humanity and humour. It's a high-pressure environment, so staying level-headed and in control is a must – and I always make sure to tell people when they've done a good job.

It's also incredibly important to encourage the sharing of creative culinary ideas at all levels, so everyone gets a seat at the table. This not only motivates the team, but also stimulates innovation and drives abilities forward. A culture built on creativity and experimentation helps progress talent in the kitchen and develop the top chefs of the future.

Glasgow is an incredible place for any chef to hone their craft. If it's not good enough, Glaswegians will be quick to tell you! They're brilliant to cater for and are fun, diverse and know what they want. It must be good; you can't fool them. For me, that's what it's all about – seeing our guests leave Crossbasket Castle's dining room with satisfied smiles on their faces after indulging in something special.

Lightly smoked sea trout, rhubarb ponzu, rice cracker, oyster creme, trout caviar

Ingredients

Sea trout

Sea trout - Med/large. 1 side of, pin-boned and skin removed

Sea salt - 200g

Golden caster sugar - 140g

Oyster creme

Oyster flesh - 50g. Reserve the oyster juice

Flat parsley - 9g. Roughly chopped

Rapeseed oil - 75g

Rhubarb ponzu

Tamari shoyu - 62ml

Mirin - 50ml

Rhubarb juice - 50ml

Lemon juice - 12ml

Lime juice - 12ml

Rice wine vinegar - 18ml

Rhubarb - 50g. Roughly chopped

Rice crackers

Jasmine rice - 100g

Sea salt

Ultratex

Togarashi spices

Garnish

Trout caviar - 2 tsp. Best quality trout caviar

Sea purslane - 4 Stems of Sea Purslane, blanched in boiling water and refreshed in ice

Iced rhubarb - 1 stick. Cut into sections and peeled or sliced on a Japanese mandolin so you have thin stick like slices store in ice for an hour or so until it crisps up and curls

Method

Serves 4

Sea trout For the trout cure, mix the salt and sugar well, liberally sprinkle half on a tray, lay the fish on top of the cure mix, sprinkle the remainder of the salt/sugar mix on top of the fish. Cling film and refrigerate for 3.5 hours to cure. When done, rinse and pat dry totally. For the best results cold smoke over smoking chips, depending on your set up use a steamer tray over a gastro on the solid top, a smoking gun and inject the smoke under a wrapping of cling film, or a pellet smoker, let the smoke permeate for a minimum of 60 mins, take out, trim the fatty belly and chill to firm up.

Oyster creme Blend the herbs and oyster on full speed. Slowly add the oil to emulsify as if making a mayonnaise. Season with lime juice to taste. Add the remaining oyster liquid to thin out the emulsion to your liking.

Rhubarb ponzu Mix all the ingredients together and infuse for 12 hours or overnight with the rhubarb trimmings. Once infused, pass through a chinois and transfer to a squeeze bottle.

Rice crackers Wash the rice well under running water. Cook in boiling water for 25 mins or until over cooked. Drain, reserving 200g of the cooking liquor. Blend the cooked rice and reserved water until a smooth puree is achieved. If you can, add a large pinch Ultratex.

Spread on dehydrator mats and dehydrate overnight at 65°C until dry and snaps. Store in a clean dry tub until needed. Deep fry at 220°C for 5 secs or until puffed. Drain on kitchen paper and season with sea salt and a pinch of togarashi spices.

To assemble Cut 5 neat 2mm slices of the trout and arrange as per the photo. Dress the trout with the oyster crème, the curled rhubarb pieces and broken pieces of rice cracker. Garnish this with the sea purslane and using the small edge of a teaspoon some pearls of the caviar. Pour over some of the chilled ponzu.

< Lightly smoked sea trout, rhubarb ponzu, rice cracker, oyster creme, trout caviar

Tomato tart, chilled tomato consomme, onion soubise, bonnet goats cheese

Ingredients

Tart cases -
Makes around 6 small tarts

Plain flour - 100g

Parmesan - 40g

Cold butter - 42g

Egg yolk - 1

Tomatoes

Your choice of tomatoes - See tomato preparation for guide

Tomato water for consomme

Ripe vine tomatoes - 1.5kg for 6 tarts

Chopped roughly

Sea salt - 1 tsp

Celery salt - Large pinch

Garlic cloves - 4. Smashed

Basil leaves - 6. Torn

Thyme - 2 stalks. Rubbed and smashed

Caster sugar - 1/2 tsp

Onion soubise

White onions - 500g. Sliced

Cream - 75g

Olive oil

Rosemary - 1 sprig

Goats cheese

Scottish Bonnet goats cheese - 50g. Trim the cheese of rinds and freeze until ready

Aliums

Chive flowers - A handful

Goats curd

Whipped curd - 20g. Put in a piping bag, set aside

Method

Tart cases Place all the ingredients except the yolk in mixer with the paddle attachment. Mix until breadcrumb consistency. Add yolk and combine. Rest overnight. We use 4cm diameter, fluted tart moulds. Roll out the dough with a pasta machine if you have one. Roll around 2mm thick. Place in the tarts leaving an overlap, pressing in and thinning out the dough a little. Dock the tarts with a fork to help them not puff up. Put the tart cases inside each other as a stack. Bake with a small tray on top weighted down (to again stop puffing) at 165°C until lightly coloured. Allow to cool. Once cold and firm, shave the overhang with a micro plane to tidy the tart edges up.

Tomato preparations You can fill the tarts with as many or as few tomatoes as you wish. We use a combination of different preparations and textures for the tomato so, really, this is up to you. For yellow tomatoes we cut raw into chunks – dress with a little good olive oil and sea salt. For green tomatoes repeat but season with smoked sea salt. For the red and yellow cherry tomatoes we semi dry, cut in half and season with oil and sea salt and some torn basil leaves – leave somewhere warm until they start to shrivel. If you have a dehydrator this is ideal. For tomato powder, slice left over tomatoes and place on oiled baking parchment. Again leave somewhere warm or in a dehydrator until they are dry and crisp, takes around 2 – 3 days. Blend in a grinder until you have a fine powder, this can be used for lots of other things as a seasoning.

Tomato water Blend everything into a runny paste and pour into a colander lined with muslin. Fold over the cloth so the mix is enveloped. Refrigerate and allow to drip through overnight. Avoid weighting so the water doesn't cloud. Keep chilled. We sometimes boost the flavour with some drops of tomato yuzu ponzu to heighten the flavours. Up to you to experiment.

Onion soubise In a pan drizzle in a little oil and gently sweat down the onions with the rosemary until they slowly caramelize. When nice and golden brown add the cream and simmer until the cream is reduced by 50%. Reduce the mix by 1/4. Allow to cool. Remove the herbs and blend until very smooth. If grainy pass through a drum sieve. Bottle up in plastic squeeze bottles or into a piping bag. Keep chilled.

To assemble Use a separate tray and place the tart on the tray. Pipe a little onion soubise in the base and top with goats curd around halfway up the tart. Arrange the different tomato preparations neatly as per the picture. Pipe a few small dots of onion soubise around the sides. The idea is to have different types and colours of the tomato visible. Prepare the tomato consommé. If you are using – flavour the water with some Tomato Yuzu Ponzu (if making for a vegetarian omit as it contains fish) but do try and experiment as this really raises the flavour profiles. Microplane the bonnet goats cheese over the tarts until you have some good height. Dress the tarts with the chive flowers. In a bowl pipe a little leftover goats curd in the middle so the tart does not slide around. Place the tart on this. Pour the consomme into serving jugs to add at the table.

< Tomato tart, chilled tomato consomme, onion soubise, bonnet goats cheese

Page 92 Treacle cured scotch beef, haggis, onion, truffle and hazelnut salsa

Treacle cured Scotch beef, haggis, onion, truffle and hazelnut salsa

Ingredients

Beef fillet

Scotch Beef Fillet - 800g. Centre/ Barrel Cut

Marmite

Black treacle

Broccoli purée

Broccoli - 2 large heads

Water

Salt

Haggis faggot

Chicken breast - 75g. Diced

Cream - 62ml

Egg white - 1/2. 25g

Salt - Large pinch

Haggis - 150g. Crumbled

Pigs caul fat/crepinette - soaked for 1 hour in cold running water

Onions

Roscoff onions - 2. Medium to Large

Onion caramel

White onions - 1kg. Finely Shredded

Salt - 50g

Thyme - 2 large sprigs

Sherry vinegar

Method

Beef fillet Brush the beef fillet with marmite, then rub black treacle all over the beef fillet and tightly cling film, pulling into a tight cylinder and tie off both ends so the fillet doesn't unravel.

Tightly vac-pac and leave for 2 days. On the morning of the day you are cooking, cook the beef in the bag in a water bath for 50 mins at 54°C.

Broccoli purée Large pan of water, measure the amount of water and add 3% of Salt. Cut down the flowery part to the stems only to 5mm (needs all flowery parts). Boil in salted water and drain, refresh in iced water.

Blitz very well – helps to smooth the puree and bring out the green chlorophyll. Pass through a drum sieve over an iced bowl. Check seasoning.

Haggis faggot Make the chicken mousse by blending the chicken breast well, add the egg and blend. Add the cream and salt and blend again until smooth. Pass through a drum sieve over an iced bowl. Check seasoning.

Add the crumbled haggis. Mix well and roll into weighed 30g balls. Chill until firm and then wrap in one layer of caul and cling film the balls. Tie off the long end of the cling film with a knot. Poach in simmering water for 5 mins, remove and chill in ice until cold and firm. Remove the film and dry.

Onions Peel the onions and in a medium low oven roast until the onion heart is softened but not mushy.

Onion caramel Mix the salt, thyme and onions and vacuum bag . Steam for 3 – 4 hours. Allow to cool and squeeze the onions hard until all the juice is out. Pass the juice and weigh 1/4 the amount of sugar to juice. ie. 500ml onion juice needs 125g sugar. Make a direct caramel with the sugar – adding the sugar bit by bit. Add the onion juice, taking care it doesn't splash or foam up, reduce to a syrup, add a good splash of sherry vinegar at the end.

Red wine jus Caramelize the shallots and mushrooms in separate pans, then deglaze with vinegar. Add stocks together and reduce by 1/4. Pour over the mushroom and shallots and cook out till sauce consistency is reached.

Port wine shallots Put the shallots into a pan and pour over enough Port to cover them. Simmer until the liquid has all but evaporated. Cool.

Hazelnut truffle salsa Mix the oil, hazelnuts and microplaned truffle together.

Ingredients

Red wine jus

Button mushrooms - 250g. Sliced

Shallots - 125g. Sliced

Bay leaf - 1/2

Thyme - 1 sprig

Pepper corns - 2

Red wine - 500ml. Reduced to 250ml

Veal jus - 500ml

Chix stock - 500ml

Cabernet sauvignon vinegar - 100ml

Port wine shallots

Shallots - 3 large. Very finely diced

Hazelnut truffle salsa

Summer truffle - Small piece. Microplaned

British rapeseed truffle oil - 50ml

Hazelnuts - 20g. Roasted and Chopped

To assemble

Place the beef back in the bath at 50°C for 40 mins. Taking real care heat a non stick thick bottomed pan and drizzle in a thin film of oil. Unwrap the beef carefully and season all over with sea salt. Sear the beef all over in the hot oil taking care as it will split.

Add a little butter and let it foam. Then add some treacle and keep basting and rolling the beef until you have a great shine and its very sticky all over.

Take your time with this – it's worth the focus. Then place in the oven until you have your desired cooking temp.

We keep the beef nice and pink – so 170°C for 6 – 8 mins is fine, allow to rest for 8 – 10 mins on a cooling rack with a tray underneath. When ready to plate cut into 4 equal portions.

In a small non stick pan wipe with oil and add a small knob of good butter and allow to foam.

Cook the onion face down until golden brown, add some onion caramel and allow to bubble until sticky and well glazed, keep warm.

In another small non stick pan wipe with oil and add a small knob of good butter and a thyme sprig and allow to foam, add the haggis balls and colour all over, finish in the oven for 3 mins.

Warm the Broccoli puree. It does not need to be red hot as it will thicken and grain.

Warm the sauce and add a large spoon of the port wine shallots.

With all the ingredients warm and ready you can plate as per the picture.

> Manjari 64% chocolate, tamarind whip, sponge, citrus caramel

Manjari 64% chocolate, tamarind whip, sponge, citrus caramel

Ingredients

Soft flex ganache

Gelatine leaf - 2 Sheets
Whipping cream (1) - 300g
Glucose syrup - 70g
Agar-agar - 2g
Dark Manjari 64% chocolate - 130g

Hazelnut coral sponge

Egg Whites - 125g
Egg Yolks - 80g
Hazelnuts - 60g. Toasted
Plain Flour - 20g
Caster Sugar - 70g

Citrus caramel

Caster Sugar - 60g
Whipping cream - 60g
Glucose - 40g
Butter - 30g
White Opalys Valrhona chocolate - 60g
Orange - 1. Zested
Lemon - 1. Zested

Tamarind whip

Whipping cream (2) - 120g
Glucose - 30g
Tamarind paste - 50g
Gelatine sheets - 2
White chocolate - 150g
Whipping cream (2) - 300g

Chocolate tuiles

Egg whites - 30g
Melted butter - 30g
Plain flour - 20g
Caster sugar - 30g
Cocoa powder - 10g

Chocolate tuiles

Viola flowers
Micro lemon balm
Toasted hazelnut halves
Orange segments

Method

Soft flex ganache Bloom the gelatine in iced water until soft, squeeze out excess water. Set aside. Heat the cream (1), agar-agar, and glucose in a pan, bring to a full boil. Take off the heat and stir in gelatine until melted. Pour the cream mix over the choc and mix until combined. Pour into lined moulds and chill for 2 hours. Cut out into 80mm rounds and cut another round in the middle with a 50mm cutter. Set aside.

Hazelnut coral sponge Place all the ingredients in a blender and blend until smooth. Strain the mix through a fine sieve. Place in an espuma gun with 2 charges. Shake the gun well and extrude into paper cups halfway up. Microwave for 1 min on full power and leave to cool at room temp.

Citrus caramel Prepare a direct dry caramel with the sugar – cook to 170°C. Heat the cream and glucose and stir into the caramel, add butter and mix until combined. Pour caramel over chocolate and stir until combined. Stir in the zests. Set aside for assembly.

Tamarind whip Soak gelatine in iced water until soft. Remove and squeeze dry. Set aside. Bring cream, glucose and tamarind to the boil. Add gelatine and stir in until melted. Pour the cream over the chocolate and stir until melted. Stir in cream (2) and set in chiller for 1 hour. Whip to soft peaks in a kitchen aid mixer.

Chocolate tuiles Combine all the ingredients in a bowl and mix to a smooth paste. Spread evenly on a silicone mat. Bake at 160°C for 8 mins. Cool and break into shards.

To assemble Place the flex ganache on the plate as per the picture. Pipe dots of the tamarind whip directly onto the ring. Break up the sponge and add to the ring, pipe some random spots of caramel onto the ring. Garnish with the toasted hazelnuts, violas, and lemon balm. Place around the orange segments then the tuile shards.

10 Cail Bruich
Lorna McNee
Chef director

At 16, while still at school, I wanted to earn some pocket money, so I got a job as a kitchen porter (KP) in an Italian restaurant in my hometown. After I left school, I was unsuccessful in getting into photography school. The chef at the restaurant where I was KP encouraged me to cook, and I found I really enjoyed it.

Later, I moved to Perthshire to work as an apprentice at Andrew Fairlie's renowned fine dining restaurant where I stayed for twelve years before I came to Cail Bruich where I'm Chef Director.

Cail Bruich is a friendly fine dining restaurant where we put the guest first with simple furnishings and a calm, relaxing ambience where we serve fantastic produce. We take great produce and let it sing enhanced with a light touch and fantastic sauces which capitalises on the best food Scotland has to offer.

Sauces are very important to me and really finish off a dish. We take great time and care at Cail Bruich into making them and there is a lengthy process. We start by making sure we make a great stock, then we incorporate that into the building of our sauces with alcohol and interesting seasonings.

Seasonality is so important as you get the best of flavours from the produce when in season. February to August in Scotland is best for wild herbs and berries while August onwards is game season, and we tend to use more game over the winter.

I feel that people are eating far more healthily than before, therefore we like to reflect that in our food with trying to make sure we have a lightness of touch throughout. There is an eight-course tasting menu served at Cail Bruich, so we need to ensure that we balance the menu well. We like to start fresh and vibrant then continue into a deeper and richer feel.

At Cail Bruich we're all a family to each other and enjoy what we do serving great food to our guests. In the kitchen as Chef Director, you've got to be disciplined and robust when you need to but also friendly and approachable. That's how you get the best out of your team.

It's a great honour to be the only female chef in Scotland with a Michelin star. It was also fantastic when Cail Bruich became the first restaurant in Glasgow for some time to be awarded a Michelin star. What was really satisfying was to see the support we got in social media and the press for receiving the award. It was as if we'd got it for Glasgow, not just for Cail Bruich. It was nice to achieve that for the city.

There has been massive progress in the food scene in Glasgow with different cultures in the city which is always welcome. It's a city full of character and I love working in a challenging and highly satisfying environment at Cail Bruich.

"We take great produce and let it sing enhanced with a light touch"

Isle of Wight tomato, crab, raw scallop and tomato consomme

Ingredients

Tomato consomme

Cherry Isle of Wight vine tomatoes - 200g
Strawberries - 10g
Basil - 1 sprig
Lemon grass - 1 stick
Fresh elderflower - 1 sprigs
Elderflower vinegar - 10ml
Elderflower cordial - 10ml
Celery - 1 stick
Cucumber - 100g
Shallot - 1/2
Garlic - 1/4 clove
Salt
Good quality olive oil

Demi dried tomatoes

Vine plum Isle of Wight tomato - 10
Tomato ponzu - 40ml
Mirin - 40ml
Soy - 20ml
Sambizu - 20ml
Shio koji - 10ml
SushiSushi smoked vinegar - 15ml
Minus 8 vinegar - 20ml
Early royal olive oil - 60ml

Crab and scallop

Brown cock crab - 2 large
Scallops - 20 large. In shell
Protein glue - 50g

For plating

Scottish strawberries - 6
Tomato petals - 6
Katy Rodgers creme fraiche
Basil cress
Marjoram
Wildflowers

Method

Serves 4

Tomato consomme Dice all ingredients and put in a large bowl, mix well and season with a little bit of salt.

Clingfilm bowl tightly and place over a simmering bowl of water. Keep over this bain marie for 2 hours.

Strain through muslin and season with salt, vinegar and cordial if needed.Before serving, add some olive oil for body and flavour.

Demi dried tomatoes Take the eye out of the tomato and score on the bottom. Blanch in boiling water and refresh.

Remove skin and seeds. Reserve skin and seeds for later. Semi dry in the oven at 100°C for 4 hours.

Mix all wet ingredients together and emulsify. Place tomatoes in this liquor and marinade for 1 week before use.

Take the seeds and skins from the tomatoes and cook in a pan until thick. Lay this on a tray and dry overnight at 80°C. The next day, cool this mix and then blend and add salt. This seasoning is used on the crab later.

Crab and scallop Shuck the scallops, wash the meat, and then place on a tray with a cloth.

Dust all the scallops in the protein glue and then roll into a large ballotine.

Freeze the ballotine and then slice thinly on a meat slicer and dress in olive oil. Reserve in freezer until ready to use.

Kill crab and remove claws. Steam claws at 72°C for 7 mins. Remove meat from claw and pick crab so there is no shell remaining.

When ready to plate, season the crab with tomato salt and the scallop with olive oil and sea salt.

To finish Dice fresh red strawberries and tomatoes and mix. Dice some basil and add to the mix, season with the marinade from the tomatoes.

Place a small amount of creme fraiche onto the bowl, put crab meat on top of that then place the green strawberries on and around the crab.

Encase the crab and strawberries in a disc of the raw scallop. Season the chilled Consommé with some of the tomato petal marinade. Pour the chilled tomato consommé around the bowl. Garnish the top of the scallop with cresses and wildflowers.

< Isle of Wight tomato, crab, raw scallop and tomato consomme

Roast turbot, langoustine XO sauce, lime

Ingredients

XO sauce

Sundried tomatoes not in oil - 100g. Wellocks

Red Chilli - 10g

Oil - 100g

Shrimp XO paste - 10g

Confit shallot

Shallot - 1 large

Chardonny vinegar - 100g

White balsamic vinegar - 100g

Langoustine bisque

Langoustine heads and claws - 2kg

Carrot - 1 small

Shallot - 1 small

Celery - 1 small

Garlic - 1 clove

Fennel - 1/4 bulb

Tomato puree - 20g

White wine - 100ml

Pernod - 50ml

Brandy - 50ml

Basil - 1 sprig

Plum tomato - 1

Cream - 200ml

Butter - 100g

Turbot brine

Turbot - 400g piece

Salt - 50g

Water - 500g

Turbot glaze

Honey - 150g

Lime - 20g

Lemon - 20g

Grapefruit - 20g

Orange - 20g

Stir fry

Celeriac - 200g

Carrot - 200g

Ginger - 20g

Lime - 1. Juiced

Coriander - 10g. Picked

Sesame oil

Method

Serves 4

XO sauce Blend the sundried tomatoes, the red chilli and oil together in the thermos at 70°C for 7 mins.

Strain through chinois and reserve oil. Mix together with the shrimp paste in a bowl.

Confit shallot and langoustine bisque Roast Lango heads and claws at 200°C for 20 mins.

Cut vegetables to a medium dice and then roast in oil in a pan. Add tomato puree and cook out. Add in white wine and reduce to a syrup. Once wine is at a syrup, add Pernod, flame and reduce. Then add brandy, flame and reduce.

Add in the browned langoustines and smash them to expose all the flavor. Cover in water and cook for 20 mins. Add the tomatoes and basil and cook for a further 20 mins. Pass through a muslin and then reduce until intense.

Add cream and reduce again. Then add in butter and blend. Season with XO paste and blend well. Add in confit shallot and chopped pasley.

Turbot brine Dissolve the salt in the water. Brine turbot for 10 mins in brine then let sit in the fridge air drying on a wire rack.

Turbot glaze Caramelize honey and then deglaze with the citrus. Cook down and reduce until is thick and syrupy. Once the turbot is cooked, use this glaze generously over the top of the fish.

Stir fry Thinly slice the Celeriac and Carrot. Then cut into thin strands – julienne. In a large based pan, place the sesame oil, once it is smoking hot, drop in the carrot and celeriac. Season with salt, stir fry fast. Deglaze the pan with the lime juice and then mix through the coriander just before serving.

For plating Place a small amount of the stir fry in the middle of the plate, spoon plenty of the sauce around it, and then place the fish on top to finish.

< Roast turbot, langoustine XO sauce, lime

Venison, beetroot and celeriac

Ingredients

Venison farce

Pork mince - 100g
Pork fat - 50g
Venison trim - 200g
Chicken livers - 100g
Onion - 1/4. Finely bruinosed
Garlic - 1 clove
Brandy - 50g
Maderia - 50g
Port - 50g
Egg - 1 yolk
Roe deer - 1 loin

Celeriac and horseradish puree

Celeriac - 1
Colmans creamed horseradish - 50g
Whole milk - 500g
Butter - 50g
Lemon - 1

Beetroot

Ruby Beetroot - 2 Large
Rosemary - 1 sprig
Sherry vinegar - 50g
Beetroot juice - 100g
Garlic - 1 clove
Olive oil - 10ml
Ultratex - 5g

Method

Serves 4

Venison farce Sweat off onions and garlic with salt. Add in the brandy, flame and reduce to syrup. Add in the madeira, flame and reduce to syrup. Add in brandy and reduce until onions are dry. Place in fridge to cool.

Cold Smoke the pork fat for 30 mins in a Bradley smoker. Season livers well with pink salt and sear hard in a pan. Put in fridge to cool.

Mince venison, smoked pork fat and cold livers. Place in a bowl and mix in the onions, pork mince and the eggs. This will then get spread on top of the venison loin and rolled into a ballotine.

Poach venison at 48°C for 1 hour. Roast in a pan and finish with beurre noisette.

Celeriac and horseradish puree Peel and dice celeriac. Place in a pan and cover with milk. Generously season and allow to cook until soft. Pass off celeriac and then blend in the Thermomix. Add butter, horseradish and lemon juice to Thermo whilst blending. Add some of the milk if needed to create glossy puree.

Beetroot Add all the ingredients together and mix well. Wash the beetroots and then place in a bag with liquor and cook sous vide for 1 hour at 90°C. Remove from the steamer and let cool.

Take one of the beetroots and slice finely to create a little hat. Cut this out with a fluted cutter. And compress back in the cooking liquor. With the remainder of the beetroots, dice into even size dice. With 1/3 of the beetroots de-dydrate until semi chewy. This usually takes about 2 hours at 70°C depending on size diced.

Another 1/3 will get smoked in the Bradley smoker for 20 mins. The last 1/3 will be kept as they are.

Thicken some of the beetroot cooking liqour with a small amount of ultratex to use on the beetroot hat.

Reserve these for later when plating.

Confit onion

Onion - 1
Duck fat - 20g
Unsalted butter - 20g
Thyme - 1 sprig

Kampot pepper sauce

Shallot - 1/2
Carrot - 1/2
Celery - 1/2 stick
Venison trimmings - 100g
Red wine - 250g
Brandy - 250g
TrueFoods reduced veal stock - 250g
Cracked salted kampot peppercorns - 10

Confit onion Put the duck fat and butter in a wide based pan and start to melt very slowly. Slice the onions finely and place in the pan with the oil. Add salt and start to cook slowly. Once the onions are very soft, take off the heat and drain through a colander.

Pick some thyme leaves and mix this through the onion and then reseason.

Kampot pepper sauce Put a heavy based pan on a medium to high heat with some vegetable oil in it.

Dice venison into small pieces and roast in the pan with some salt. Dice all the vegetables. Once you begin to see the venison caramelize in the pan then add the vegetables and begin to let them caramelize.

Deglaze with brandy and skim. Reduce this to a syrup. Add red wine and skim. Reduce this by half. Add in veal stock and bring up to a simmer. Add in 10 of the kampot peppercorns and let infuse. Pass the sauce through muslin.

For plating With all the diced beetroots, mix them together. Add the celeriac puree and confit onion through this.

Take the beetroot hat and stuff with this filling. Fold it over and dress with the thickened beetroot liquor. Decorate with some oregano.

Carve the venison and season with good quality sea salt.
Pour the sauce into the middle of the plate.

Page 102 Venison, beetroot and celeriac

> Lemon, honey, salted milk ice cream

Lemon, honey, salted milk ice cream

Ingredients

Lemon curd

Whole eggs - 100g
Lemon zest - 1 lemon
Lemon juice - 70g
Sugar - 100g
Unsalted butter - 120g. Good quality butter

Bergamot gel

Bergamot juice - 100g
Water - 50g
Sugar - 20g
Agar agar - 3g

Lavendar honey

Runny Honey - 100g
Dried lavender - 10g

Honey cremuex

Honey - 50g
Whole milk - 150g
Gelatine - ½ sheet
Butter - 50g. Good quality butter
Cornflour - 8g

Salted milk ice cream

Double cream - 150g
Milk - 200g
Condensed Milk - 100g
Castor Sugar- 35g
Salt - Pinch
Ice-cream stabilizer - 2g

Tuille mix

Icing sugar - 50g
Egg white - 50g
Plain flour - 50g
Melted butter - 50g

Method

Serves 4

Lemon curd Into a Thermomix, put eggs, lemon juice and zest and sugar and cook to 83°C. Remove from the Thermomix and sieve out the lemon zest. Whisk or blend in the butter with no heat.

Let set for 6 – 12 hours and then set in a mould and freeze hard before popping out.

Once ready to serve, pop out the mould, dust with lemon sherbert and place on plate to defrost.

Bergamot gel Put all ingredients into a pan and boil. Remove from pan into a container and store in the fridge until set. Blend to smooth fluid gel consistency.

Lavendar honey Warm the honey and add in the dried lavender. Allow to infuse for 20 mins and then pass through a fine sieve.

Honey cremuex Warm milk. Caramelise the honey in a high based pan. Deglaze the honey with the warm milk. Make sure all the honey has dissolved and then leave this to infuse for 20 mins.

Add the cornflour and allow to boil for 1 min until fully cooked out. Add in ready soaked gelatine and then emulsify the butter into this. Allow to set in fridge and then blend to smooth texture. Place in a piping bag.

Salted milk ice cream Boil the milk and cream together. Mix sugar and stabilizer together and add to the milk mix and boil for 1 min. Add the condensed milk and boil for a further minute.

Store for 24 hours in the fridge and the freeze hard and churn in Paco Jet or churn immediately in the ice cream machine.

Tuille mix Mix all ingredients together until smooth with a whisk. Spread onto honeycomb moulds and then bake in the oven for 8 mins at 160°C. Remove from mould and cut into small circle.

For plating Put the set lemon curd onto the middle of the plate, fill the holes on the bergamot gel, honey cremuex and some olive oil. Put roche of the ice cream onto the lemon curd, then top it with the tuille. Finish with some lemon cress and then a drizzle of the warm lavender honey.

11

La Lanterna
Luca Conreno
Owner and head chef

"I look upon the chef as an artist who takes a simple product and creates an edible, beautiful dish."

My mother's family had a farm in a village outside Turin with a small restaurant where they would sell food and wines to passing trade. I loved the taste and smells and developed a passion for food. So, I enrolled in catering college when I was fourteen.

For the next few years, I worked in a variety of restaurants and hotels throughout Italy. I loved working in catering and hospitality and never wanted to do anything else. Later, I worked on cruise liners where I met my wife who came from the town of Airdrie outside Glasgow.

I moved to Scotland in 1994 and after getting married in 1996, I started working in La Lanterna and I've been here ever since.

From the beginning my aim was to make La Lanterna a top-level restaurant, the perfect Italian restaurant outside of Italy. We put a lot into transforming what was an old fashion Italian restaurant. I also frequently use social media and make videos about Italian food to promote the restaurant, and I recently featured on a food programme on Scottish Television.

I would describe La Lanterna as a traditional Italian restaurant with a willingness to adapt and try new dishes. It's vital if you're going to try new recipes that you build on a firm foundation of tradition. An Italian restaurant must be just that – Italian with the staples of lasagne, carbonara and so on as the bedrock from which you can experiment and devise new dishes and recipes.

At La Lanterna we source as much as we can from Italy – all our wines, for instance are Italian – and our meat and seafood fresh from local suppliers in Scotland. My aim is to constantly produce quality food with great service.

For me to work in cuisine you need to love and have a passion for food. I look upon the chef as an artist who takes a simple product and creates an edible, beautiful dish. Too much emphasis can be placed upon the look of a dish; that's important, sure. But flavour, the taste, is fundamental. If it doesn't taste right on the palate, all that effort on appearance is ruined.

Working as a head chef in high-pressured kitchens means you must get the balance right between cooking and the pressure to get orders out at busy times. You need to keep calm and control yourself. I often like to think of a chef in a busy kitchen as comparable to an army commander who's in front of his men guiding them, not standing to the side or behind them. Likewise, the head chef needs to get stuck in, cooking the food and doing all the other things they're asking the staff to do. And no matter how busy it gets you have to step back and still love the buzz.

I love the warmth of the people of Glasgow. I'm also impressed by how our city centre site has retained its popularity and loyal customer base over the past few decades. That's a testament to the quality and consistency of what we're serving at both La Lanterna in the city centre and our newer outlet in the West End.

I am an Italian, past, present and future with a passion for bringing the finest of Italian food to the people of Glasgow. That gives me immense satisfaction.

Vitello tonnato

Ingredients

Marinated veal

Veal eye round - 400g

Celery stick - 1

Carrot - 1

Onion - 1. Cut in half

Bay leaves - 3

Cloves - 3

Salt - 1 pinch

Water - 1l

Tonnato sauce

Tinned tuna in olive oil - 100g. Drained

Capers - 10. Drained

Anchovy fillets - 6

Mayonnaise - 200g

Lemon - 1/2. Juice

To garnish

Capers - Drained

Celery - Julienne cut

Vitello tonnato is a Piedmontese most celebrated cold dish in Italy. This dish is a masterpiece of the mix between sea and mountains. It is served in the summertime chilled or at room temperature as the main course of an Italian meal or as an elegant antipasto for an elaborate dinner.

Method

Slowly boil the meat for 40 mins with all the 'marinated veal' ingredients. Remove the meat from the liquid and allow to cool completely, after rest in the fridge for 3 hours.

Blend tuna, capers, anchovies with the juice of lemon while the meat is cooling. Add mayonnaise and gently mix to complete the sauce. Finish with pinch of black pepper.

Serve finely sliced veal on a serving dish. Spoon the sauce generously over the meat. Garnish with julienne cut celery and whole capers.

Enjoy your vitello tonnato. This dish pairs well with a crisp white wine like Gavi di Gavi or a light red like a Barbera.

< Vitello tonnato

Risotto mare and monti

Ingredients

King prawns - 8. Peeled and deveined
Monkfish - 100g. Diced
Red onion - 1/2. Finely chopped
Courgette - 1. Diced
Arborio rice - 200g
Vegetable stock - 800ml
Olive oil - 2 tbsp
Butter - 2 tbsp
Salt and pepper - To taste
Parmesan cheese - 2 tbsp. Grated
Fresh parsley - Chopped, for garnish

Risotto mare e monti elegantly fuses the finest elements of land and sea. While the classic recipe often features different ingredients, we invite you to elevate the experience with tender courgette, adding a sophisticated touch. The delicate flavours complement the rich seafood, creating a refined and refreshing twist on this Italian classic. The creamy risotto base harmoniously integrates these premium ingredients, offering a gourmet taste of Italy's culinary excellence. Perfect for those seeking a distinctive and indulgent dining experience.

Method

Sauté the vegetables and seafood Heat 2 tbsp of extra virgin olive oil in a large pan over medium heat.

Add the diced red onion and diced courgette, sautéing until the onion becomes translucent and the courgette is tender, about 5 mins.

Add the king prawns and diced monkfish to the pan. Toss everything together and cook for about 5 mins, until the prawns are pink and the monkfish is opaque. Season with salt and pepper to taste. Remove from the heat and set aside.

Toast the Rice In a separate large pot, melt 1 tbsp of butter over medium heat. Add the Arborio rice and toast it for about 1 min, stirring constantly to coat the rice in the butter.

Cook the Risotto Begin adding the warm vegetable stock to the rice, one ladleful at a time. Stir frequently, allowing the rice to absorb the stock before adding more. Continue this process for about 10 mins.

After 10 mins, gently fold in the sautéed seafood and vegetables. Continue cooking for another 10 mins, gradually adding the rest of the stock, until the rice is creamy and fully cooked.

Finish the Risotto Stir in the remaining knob of butter to add richness and creaminess. Mix in the grated Parmesan cheese, then adjust the seasoning with salt and pepper if needed.

Serve Spoon the risotto onto plates or into bowls. Garnish with freshly chopped parsley. Serve immediately and enjoy your luxurious risotto mare e monti.

< Risotto mare and monti

Page 113 Zabaglione alla Piemontese

Cervo and salsiccia

Ingredients

Venison loin - 2 x 300g medallions

Italian sausages - 2 small

Porcini mushrooms - 100 g. Cleaned and sliced

Red wine - 1/2 cup

Vegetable stock - 1/2 cup

Butter - 2 tbsp. Or a splash of olive oil

Rosemary - 1 sprig

All-purpose flour - 2 tbsp

Salt and pepper - To taste

Fresh parsley - Chopped. For garnish

Cervo e salsiccia is an elegant Italian dish that combines the rich, distinctive flavour of venison (cervo) with the savoury, spiced notes of quality sausage (salsiccia). This pairing offers a well-balanced and satisfying culinary experience, where the tender venison is complemented by the robust, seasoned sausage. Perfect for those who appreciate fine, rustic flavours with a touch of sophistication, this dish captures the essence of Italian tradition in a memorable and indulgent meal.

Method

Serves 2

Prepare the Ingredients Lightly coat the venison medallions with flour, ensuring an even layer on all sides.

Season both the venison medallions and the sausages with a pinch of salt and pepper.

Sear the Meat In a non-stick pan, heat 2 tbsp of butter or a splash of olive oil over medium heat.

Add the sprig of rosemary to the pan, allowing it to infuse the butter or oil with its aroma.

Place the venison medallions and Italian sausages in the pan. Pan-fry for 2 – 3 mins on each side, or until both sides are nicely browned.

Cook the Mushrooms Add the sliced porcini mushrooms to the pan, stirring gently to combine with the meat. Cook for another 2 – 3 mins until the mushrooms begin to soften.

Deglaze with Red Wine Pour in the red wine, ensuring it evenly covers the bottom of the pan incorporating them into the sauce.

Simmer and Reduce Add the vegetable stock to the pan, stirring to combine. Lower the heat and allow the mixture to simmer for about 10 – 15 mins, or until the sauce has reduced and thickened slightly, and the meat is cooked to your liking.

Finish and Serve Remove the sprig of rosemary from the pan. Taste the sauce and adjust the seasoning with salt and pepper if needed.

Plate the venison medallions and sausages, spooning the porcini mushrooms and red wine sauce over the top.

Garnish with freshly chopped parsley and serve immediately.

Zabaglione alla Piemontese

Ingredients

Egg yolks - 2
Whole egg - 1
Sugar - 2 tbsp
Marsala wine - 75ml
Ground cinnamon - A touch. Optional
Savoiardi biscuits (ladyfingers) - For serving
Vanilla ice cream - 4 scoops. For serving

Zabaglione alla Piemontese is a refined Italian dessert from the Piedmont region, celebrated for its elegance. This luxurious custard blends the finest egg yolks, sugar, and premium Marsala wine, whisked to a velvety perfection. it offers a sophisticated and indulgent flavour, embodying the essence of Italian culinary artistry.

Method

Prepare the mixture In a round metal bowl, combine the egg yolks, whole egg, and sugar. Whisk gently until the mixture is smooth and slightly frothy.

Gradually add the Marsala wine while continuing to whisk.

Cook the zabaglione Set the bowl over a pot of simmering water (a double boiler setup). Allow it to heat and thicken until it becomes creamy and soft, but be careful not to let it get too hot or curdle. The mixture should reach a warm, custard-like consistency.

Season and serve Once the zabaglione is ready, remove the bowl from the heat. If desired, add a touch of cinnamon for extra flavour.

Serve the zabaglione in individual glasses.

Accompany with a side of savoiardi biscuits and a scoop of vanilla ice cream for a delightful contrast.

12 Atlantic Brasserie
Michael Lawson
Head chef

When I was still at school finishing my exams, I worked as a kitchen porter (KP) in a local restaurant near where I lived in a suburb of Glasgow. There and then I fell in love with cuisine and hospitality, and I developed this passion for food from the chefs. I suppose the best way to describe it is that I was captivated by what was happening in the kitchen. Within two months I was offered a position as commis chef with an Italian restaurant (the Italian Bistro) that was opening in the West End by Ian McMaster. The head chef there and the first I worked under was Stevie Caputa who, incidentally, appeared in the first edition of Glasgow on a Plate.

Later, I worked in a series of restaurants in the city where I was able to elevate my cooking techniques, learned a lot more about the customer as well as working with good operators and amazing chefs. That set me up for working with the DRG Group, initially as Sous Chef at the Citizen outlet and over the last three years as Head Chef at their neighbouring restaurant, the Atlantic Brasserie.

Atlantic Brasserie takes a modern approach to French cooking using classic techniques, but with a contemporary twist. Classical dishes are classic for a reason, so you focus on quality ingredients and put a lot of care and effort into every process in the kitchen. That includes building up a good team of chefs around you in relation to dishes and menus with a big emphasis on attention to detail and service.

The key to my 'food philosophy' and what I hope we offer at Atlantic Brasserie is balance and inclusion. For example, as far as I'm aware, we are the only restaurant in Glasgow offering a low FODMAP diet menu for people susceptible to IBS and other gastro disorders. I've worked very closely with our dietician Lesley Reid, in developing this. Restaurant menus should not be restrictive and offer something to everyone.

Another aspect of this is as head chef I'm committed, yes, to fresh food, but also utilising everything in the kitchen to reduce waste.

My most challenging event recently was organising a Laurent Perrier Champagne evening at Atlantic Brasserie. It was a custom menu one-off night pairing champagnes with specific dishes. I worked closely with my manager, Kostas Simos and my staff on it. It was a great success. The menu was the basis for a nationwide promotion with Laurent Perrier and FT Weekend, running for a whole month. It was a success all right, but worth all the hard work from the team in the end.

I learned a lot from that evening about organisational skills, public speaking and put me in good stead for more events in the future.

It's been satisfying working with the same team at Atlantic Brasserie. We've got seven excellent chefs and a brilliant staff with a shared enthusiasm for cooking and serving good food. I'm surrounded by talent and that makes the stressful moments easier to deal with. If every small detail is being attended to then it becomes a whole lot easier.

Glasgow has come a long way in ten years. Lots of great chefs have stayed in the city and standards have shot up. There's also a lot more foodies about; the public have become more discerning and critical, so you must up your game. By the quality of the reviews we receive, Atlantic Brasserie has achieved that.

"A modern approach to French cooking with a contemporary twist"

Confit duck and ham hough presse, sauce gribiche, roasted almonds, olive oil crostini

Ingredients

Confit duck

Terrine mould - 1. Lined with greaseproof paper
Smoked ham houghs - 2
Free range duck legs - 5
Duck fat - 500g
Rosemary - 20g
Bay leaves - 3
Dried cranberries - 25g. Roughly chopped
Flat leaf parsley - 30g
Chives - 30g. Finely chopped
Chervil - 30g. Finely chopped
Honey - 100ml
Cracked black pepper - 10g
Oranges - 2. Zest and juice
Pistachios - 30g. Roughly chopped
Whole almonds - 50g. Roasted in oven for garnish
French baguette - 1. Slice fine, drizzle with olive oil and salt. Bake at 150°C until crispy

Sauce gribiche

Large egg - 1
Banana shallot - 1. Finely diced
Chervil - 10g
Parsley - 10g
Chives - 10g
Lemon - 1. Zested
Capers - 10g. Finely chopped
Cornichons - 3. Finely chopped
Mild olive oil - 150ml
Sherry vinegar - 20ml
Dijon mustard - 15g

Method

Serves 4

Confit duck Salt duck legs overnight, wash drain and pat dry. Sear duck legs in a pan until golden brown. Place in tray and cover with duck fat, rosemary and bay leaves. Place in a tin foil tray and cook in the oven at 180°C for 90 mins until meat falls off bone.

Boil ham hough in a pot of water until tender, remove and pick meat, removing any fat. Try and keep the pieces of meat as large as possible. Keep the stock as some will be needed to set the terrine.

In a mixing bowl, combine the confit duck, boiled ham, cranberries, pistachios, herbs, honey, orange juice and zest and 100ml of the leftover ham stock.

Place the mix into the lined terrine mould and press using a weight in the fridge – for at least 12 hours.

When ready to serve, remove from mould and slice into portions.

Sauce gribiche Boil the egg in water for 8 mins, cool, peel and grate. Add shallots, lemon juice and sherry vinegar into a mixing bowl and leave to macerate for 10 mins.

Add Dijon mustard to shallot mix and slowly whisk in olive oil until thick and glossy.

Fold through the grated egg and the rest of the dry ingredients. Season to taste, adding more lemon juice if need be.

To serve Add 1 slice terrine. Spoon the gribiche on the plate and add some of the roasted almonds.

< Confit duck and ham hough presse, sauce gribiche, roasted almonds, olive oil crostini

Page 120 Lemon sole with parsley, almond and caper butter

Crab, avocado and quinoa salad, with lemon mayo and radish

Ingredients

Crab mix

White crab meat - 500g. Buy from a fishmonger

Shallots - 80g. Diced

Parsley - 30g. Chopped

Chives - 30g. Chopped

Red chilli. 20g. Fine diced

Lemon juice - 60ml

Sherry vinegar - 40ml

Olive oil - 100ml

Cracked black pepper - 10g

Salt to taste

Tabasco sauce - 5ml

Avocado purèe

Avocados - 4

Lemons - 2

Mayonnaise - 100ml

Radish - 4 small. Finely sliced

Crostini - 16

Quinoa - 200g. I like tricolour

Method

Serves 4

Crab mix Pick through crab meat, checking for any leftover shells. Combine all ingredients together and season to taste.

Lemon mayo whisk 20ml lemon juice through 100ml mayo. Peel and blend avocados in a blender with the lemon juice, adding salt to taste.

Boil the quinoa in salted water, when cooked add some olive oil and chill.

To assemble in layers Using a metal mousse ring, press some of the quinoa into the bottom, followed by the avocado then the crab mix. Make sure its tightly packed so when you remove the ring it stays standing.

Garnish with some of the lemon mayo, thinly sliced radish and the crostinis.

< Crab, avocado and quinoa salad, with lemon mayo and radish

Page 121 Lemon tart with creme fraiche and champagne raspberry sauce

Lemon sole with parsley, almond and caper butter

Ingredients

Lemon sole - 1 whole. Can be purchased from fishmonger already trimmed

Unsalted butter - 40g

Capers - 20g

Flaked almonds - 20g

Parsley - 10g. Finely chopped

Lemon - 1

French fries - 1 portion

Method

Serves 1

Preheat oven to 200°C

Place a large non-stick frying pan over a medium-high heat and add 1/2 the butter. Once the butter has melted add the lemon sole skin side down and season the flesh side.

Cook for 2 mins, adjust the heat if you need to as you don't want to burn the butter.

Once the butter starts to turn golden brown (beurre noisette), add the remaining butter, the almonds, capers and parsley.

Using a spoon, baste the fish for a few mins until cooked through, add the lemon juice and leave to rest for 1 – 2 mins before plating.

Serve with French fries.

Lemon tart with creme fraiche and champagne raspberry sauce

Ingredients

Equipment needed

Baking beads

Plain flan ring - 28cm x 2.5cm

Greaseproof paper

For the filling

Lemons - 8. Juiced

Lemon zest - 2 lemons

Large eggs - 8

Double cream - 260ml

Sugar - 360g

For the pastry

Unsalted butter - 150g

Plain flour - 250g

Egg yolks - 2

Icing sugar - 100g

Extra butter and flour for lining

Egg yolk for brushing - 1

Champagne raspberry sauce

Lauren Perrier rose - 200ml

Sugar - 150g

Fresh raspberries - 100g

Crème Fraiche - 100g

Method

Serves 4

For the filling In a mixing bowl, whisk together the sugar and eggs until pale. Whisk in the cream, lemon juice and zest. Set aside while making the pastry.

For the pastry Rub the butter and flour together until you have a fine breadcrumb. Add the egg yolks and icing sugar and bring the mix together but don't overwork it. Leave the mix to rest in the fridge for at least 20 mins.

Grease and lightly flour a 28cm x 2.5cm plain flan ring, place on a baking tray that will fit in the oven. Roll out the pastry to a thickness of 3mm, and line the mould carefully pushing the pastry into the corners.

Cut out some greaseproof paper and pour the baking beads into the pastry and leave to rest for a further 20 mins before baking.

Preheat oven to 180°C and bake the tart for 20 mins or until golden brown. Remove baking beads, brush the base of the tart with the leftover egg yolk and bake for another 5 – 10 mins or until the base of the tart is golden brown.

Turn the oven down to 100°C, add the lemon filling into the tart case and bake for 30 – 40 mins until set.

Remove from oven and allow to cool before slicing.

For the sauce In a saucepan, bring the champagne and sugar to the boil and simmer for 5 mins. Remove from the heat and add the raspberries.

Blend mix in a blender until smooth and pass through a fine sieve.

To garnish the plate Add slice of lemon tart, a quinelle of creme fraiche and some of the raspberry champagne sauce.

13 The Gannet
Peter McKenna
Chef owner

"We're not just cooking a plate of food; as restaurateurs, as chefs, we're telling a story."

The Gannet is a must for food lovers and open-minded people that are interested in where their food has come from. Over the past 11 years we have cultivated a network of likeminded producers, farmers and foragers that bring us an ever-changing seasonal bounty.

I was a kid who always wanted to be a cook before I even knew what a chef was. My family are great cooks and liked to eat out in a variety of establishments that just stoked my interest in cooking and hospitality. I ended up working in a bar stacking shelves, cleaning ashtrays, pulling pints and so on.

When I was 14, I got a job in a local hotel cleaning pots and making sandwiches. I liked the buzz of it. I worked in a local Italian restaurant where I learned to make dishes such as tiramisu. That was back in the 90s' and I got the bug for hospitality, and I've never looked back.

Since setting up The Gannet I've followed the farm-to-fork ethos (as much as possible) supporting farmers, growers and foragers; these people are the backbone of our industry. Periodically, I take the team to forage for wild mushrooms or visit farms. I love when young chefs gain a respect for the ingredients when seeing how they grow as well as the time, effort, love and respect people are putting into getting the produce to the restaurant.

My job as the chef-owner is to give our guests a snapshot of what's good in Scotland at this moment in time, and vitally, supporting local artisan businesses. We're not just cooking a plate of food; as restaurateurs, as chefs, we're telling a story.

In hospitality, you're constantly faced with challenges, it's how you deal with them and bounce back. I learned my trade working in difficult kitchens from early morning to late at night, but that experience was priceless. It gives you the resilience to have a strong belief in yourself.

Funnily, when we opened The Gannet, I really thought the public would just come in. "Hello, we're here," but business was slow. I thought, "what are we doing wrong?" But I was steadfast and believed in what I was doing; this is going to work.

Luckily our hard work paid off, we got a few good reviews, won some awards then a flow of guests started to come in, but it wasn't overnight. Now, eleven years later, The Gannet's become an institution.

Kevin Dow has been at the helm front of house for ten years, absolutely rocksteady in his approach, a consummate professional who has the respect of all his team and peers.

I've got a brilliant team with a positive mindset; a lot have been here for years learning their craft. Five years down the line they're the people who're going to be leading the food scene here in Glasgow.

It's a brilliant city to work in because you know all the other operators, so there's a friendly competition.

It's been particularly good to see the tourism market change as more and more tourists are using Glasgow as their city-break destination or stopping off before exploring the west coast or the islands.

Even with all the challenges of running a hospitality business in 2024 I am optimistic. Glasgow's food scene has never been better, young passionate people are opening up eateries in every corner of the city, I can see a bright future ahead.

Cured Loch Melford sea trout, oyster cream, cucumber and apple

Ingredients

Cured sea trout

Sea trout - 1 side
Sea salt - 350g
Soft brown sugar - 175g
Dried kelp (seaweed) - 30g
Cracked black pepper - 10g
Lemons - 2. Zested
Limes - 2. Zested

Kohlrabi disks

Kohlrabi - 1. Diameter 3.1 cm
Salt brine - 2%
Dill - 2 sprigs

Cucumber

Cucumber - 1
Dill oil - 50g

Apple

Granny Smith Apple - 1
Rice wine vinegar - 50ml
White sugar - 50g
Water - 100ml

Oyster emulsion

Oyster meat - 100g. Reserve juice
Parsley - 10g
Salt - 1g
Gin - 10g
Neutral oil - 150ml
Lemon juice - 15g
Xantham - 1g
Crème fraiche - 150g

Method

This is a perfect dish to serve on a warm day, lots of punchy flavours and interesting textures, perfect with a glass of brut champagne.

Cured sea trout Blend the citrus & pepper with the sugar and salt. In a large gastro cover the fish in the cure mix, vac pack and leave in the fridge for 6 hours. Wash off carefully and dry.

Kohlrabi disks Thinly slice the kohlrabi, cut small discs using a ring mould. Add the discs to the brine and leave at room temperature for 4 – 5 days, the Kohlrabi will have fermented and taken on a pleasant sour flavour. Add the dill and refrigerate.

Cucumber Peel and dice the cucumber. Cover in the oil and leave to infuse.

Apple Dissolve the sugar in vinegar on a medium heat. Remove from the heat and add the water – chill. Dice the apple then pour the chilled pickle over and leave to infuse for a minimum of four hours before use.

Oyster emulsion Blend the oyster, parsley, salt and gin until smooth. Slowly add the oil, add juice when necessary. Add the xantham and blend to activate.

Season with lemon juice and salt if necessary, remember all oysters have different salinity – pass. Fold in the crème fraiche (might not need it all, depends on the oysters).

To serve Arrange the diced sea trout in the middle of a suitable plate. Put the oyster cream into a piping bag. Pipe dots of a cream sporadically onto the trout (so every spoonful gets some).

Add the apple, 6 – 8 pieces depending on size, spread out evenly. Top with the kohlrabi discs, again spread out evenly.

Garnish with the petals.

< Cured Loch Melford sea trout, oyster cream, cucumber and apple

Page 128 Scallops, sweet corn, girolles and greenheart micro leaves

Scottish lobster and crab cannelloni

Ingredients

Lobster

Lobster - 1. 750g
Unsalted Butter - 250g
Water - 100ml

Scallop mousse

Scallop meat - 150g
Crab meat - 80g. Picked
White of egg - 1
Double cream - 100ml
Lemon zest - 1 lemon

Pasta dough

Pasta Flour - 500g
Egg Mix (2 whole eggs the rest yolks) - 180g
Squid ink - 120g
Olive Oil - 20ml
Salt - 5g

Lobster bisque

Lobster carcasses - 3 large
Unsalted Butter - 200g
Tomato purée - 100g
Brandy - 200ml
White wine - 200ml
Fennel bulb - 1 large
Carrots - 2 large
Onion - 1 medium
Leek - 1 medium
Celery stick - 1
Garlic clove - 4
Star anise - 1
White peppercorns - 2
Bay leaf - 1

Method

Lobster Fill a pot of water and bring to the boil, season liberally (should taste of the sea). Pick out a live, heavy lobster. Put to sleep in a freezer for 20 mins. Blanch in the water for two mins. Refresh in ice water. Remove the claws and cook for a further 6 – 8 mins in the boiling water (depending on the size). Cool claws in ice water.

Remove the tail meat from the shell. Once the claws are chilled, crack with a rolling pin or back of an old knife. Gently remove the flesh. Make an emulsion with the butter and water season with salt and cracked black pepper. Gently cook the tail in the emulsion, add the claws to warm when the tail is cooked.

Scallop mousse Blend the scallop meat to a smooth paste. Add the egg white quickly. Pass through a sieve. Beat in the cream. Season with salt.

Add the picked crab meat and lemon zest. Store in a piping bag until ready to assemble the cannelloni's.

Pasta dough Form a well with the flour & salt. Mix the egg, ink and oil. Add the egg mix to the flour while mixing. Knead the dough until smooth and glossy. Ready for 1 hour in a fridge before use.

Using a pasta machine roll out the dough. Bring to 1.5 inches thickness and cut rectangles (even sizes to suite your appetite). Pipe a nice line of crab and scallop mixture. Roll into a nice tube and wrap in cling film. Tie the ends of the cling film.

Lobster bisque Thoroughly pick the meat, wash the shells, dry and smash into small pieces. Heat oil in roasting tray, add the carcass and quickly sear. Lower heat slightly add the vegetables (chopped to the same size as the carcass) and begin to caramelise. Add the butter, allow it to foam and then continue to caramelise. Add the tomato to the pan/tray, continue the caramelisation process until deep red in colour and there is a sweet aroma, being careful not to allow the mix to catch. Remove 1/3 of the mix and reserve for later. De glaze the pan with the alcohol until almost dry then just cover with water. Place in a suitable saucepan and bring to a gentle but steady simmer and allow to cook out for 20 – 25 mins. Pulse with the stick blender to crush slightly and push through a coarse colander then a fine chinois. Heat a sauce pan, add the bisque and reduce rapidly to required consistency, throw in the reserved carcass allow to cook gently for 2 mins, then remove from heat and allow to infuse for 5 – 8 mins with a couple of pinches of tarragon (optional). Pass through a fine chinois twice. For 150ml bisque add 80ml semi skimmed milk and two knobs of good butter. Bring to the boil and blend with a hand blender.

To serve Firstly put a suitable pot of water on for the cannelloni. Bring to the boil then down to simmer. Cook the cannelloni for 4 mins. Remove from the water and cut one end then slide the pasta out.

When the lobster is cooked remove from the emulation, trim up and season with sea salt and lemon juice. Plate the lobster, then the cannelloni. Foam up the bisque with a hand blender and sauce generously.

< Scottish lobster and crab cannelloni

Page 129 Hazelnut and dark chocolate choux, hazelnut gelato

Scallops, sweet corn, girolles and greenheart micro leaves

Ingredients

Scallops - 8 XL. In their shell. Ask your fishmonger to open the scallops and discard the skirt and sacks. Reserve the roe for another dish.

Sweet corn

Corn kernels - 250g. Cooked

Chicken stock - 250g

Salt

Girolles/garlic and parsley butter

Girolles - 100g

Salted butter - 200g. Good quality

Flat-leaf parsley - 30g. Picked

Greenheart micro leaves - 30g.

Garlic - 4 cloves

Herb oil

Parsley - 200g

Chives - 150g

Sunflower oil - 400ml

Salt - 6g

Method

Scallops Wash and dry the scallops, and leave to firm up on J-cloth.

Sweet corn Finely chop the sweetcorn and put it Into a hot pan with some butter, cook till sizzles. Add the stock and Bring to the boil. Once the corn is tender blend it Into a smooth puree. Season pass through a sieve.

Girolles Scrape the mushrooms clean and rinse under a tap of running water. Dry in some kitchen paper.

Garlic and parsley butter Bring the butter to room temp. Blend all the ingredients well. Form into a log with cling film. Refrigerate.

Herb oil Blend all the ingredients in the thermomix at 80°C. Strain through a cloth and immediately chill over ice. Carefully remove the solidified oil and discard the frozen liquid. Refrigerate until needed.

To serve Pan fry the scallops, finish with some diced chilled butter. (I like to cook them medium rare).

Gently Cook the girolles in garlic butter.

Heat the corn and spoon onto the plate as you see fit. Slice the scallops in half and arrange nicely. Scatter on the girolles and some butter. Add a little herb oil. Garnish wth the micro cress .

Hazelnut and dark chocolate choux, hazelnut gelato

Ingredients

Choux pastry

Milk - 100g
Water - 100g
Salt - 2g
Sugar - 2g
Butter - 90g
All-purpose flour - 110g
Whole egg - 200g
Soft butter - 35g
Cane sugar - 45g
Flour - 45g
Whole egg - 1. Beaten

Crumble topping

Butter - 35g
Sugar - 35g
Flour - 45g

Praline ganache

Whipping cream - 150g
Hazelnut praliné - 50g
Dark chocolate - 150g

Hazelnut praliné Ice cream

Almond milk - 330g
Coconut milk - 68g
Sugar - 5g
Trimoline (invert sugar) - 8g
Atomized glucose - 13g
Ice cream stabilizer - 5g
50% praline - 100g
Total mass (1 Pacojet bowl) - 529g

Method

The choux is a classic that deserves its place on menus up and down the country only if executed well. When done right it's a thing of beauty. When not... Well we all know the score.

Preheat the oven to 230°C.

For the choux Bring the milk and water with 90g of butter to the boil. Mix the flour with the salt and 2g sugar. Remove from the heat, add 110g flour all at once and quickly mix in. This should immediately form a solid batter.

Cook over low heat until the batter detaches from the edge and looks dry. Stir frequently with a spatula. Remove from the heat and add the eggs one by one. With each egg you add, stir the batter again until homogeneous.

Prepare a piping bag and add the mix. Pipe the batter onto a silicone-matted baking tray and then freeze.

For the crumble topping Mix 35g butter, cane sugar and 45g flour in the mixing bowl using a spatula. Roll out into an even dough of about 2mm. Cut out the dough into small circles just slightly smaller than the choux dough.

Brush with beaten egg and cover the puffs with the circles of dough. Place the puffs in the oven and turn the temperature down to 170°C, the fan should be on the very lowest setting. Bake the choux for 15 – 20 mins.

Praliné ganache Bring the cream to boiling point. Pour 100g of the cream onto the chocolate. Mix with a hand-held blender until you have a smooth paste. Now add the remaining cream and blend until you have a smooth homogeneous mixture. Cover the ganache and leave it to rest in the refrigerator for at least 2 hours.

Hazelnut praliné Ice cream Mix the sugar, atomized glucose with the ice stabilizer. Heat the almond milk with the coconut cream and invert sugar to 50°C. Add the powders, mix and boil.

Pour over the praline and emulsify like a ganache.

Mix in a hand blender and freeze in a paco bowl or churn in ice cream machine.

To serve Once the ganache is chilled put into a piping bag with a star nozzle. Cut the puffs in half through the centre.

Neatly spoon the ice cream into the centre of the puffs. Surround the ice cream with stars of the ganache. Top the choux and serve.

14

Margo
Robin Aitken
Head chef

I started out in the dining trade at 16 when I left school and my mother, who was a college lecturer in languages at City of Glasgow College, was tired of me lounging around the house. She got me enrolled in a chef's course at the college. My mother was pushing at an open door as I'd always enjoyed cooking; it had been my main task around the house growing up. It helped that I'd always loved cooking and I really enjoyed watching TV programmes like Ready Steady Cook and people like Ainsley Harriot and Richard Corrigan. I was excited with the possibilities of what you could do with food and cooking.

I moved to Australia in my mid-20s, finding my feet and learning to adapt to a new culture. I found that quite challenging. But I learned to be confident in your own abilities. Basically no one's going to know your good unless you prove it.

The restaurant, Margo that I'm head chef of, is in Glasgow city centre. We want it to be an exciting place for people who really enjoy food and to celebrate. I want to attract people who like to try new styles of food and ingredients. One of the things we're really focusing on at Margo is sourcing and getting new things on the menu.

If asked what my 'food philosophy' is, I would say it's very much ingredient focused, but also based on simplicity. I think food should be cooked in a classic way, super fresh, seasonal (I'm passionate about seasonality), colourful and exciting as possible while also being straightforward and not overthinking it. Basically, it's not about the person cooking, it's all about the food.

One of my most challenging experiences was in a bar/diner in New Zealand when I was in my twenties. Every other member of staff walked out the bar except for me and a waitress who came downstairs to help me with the dishes as I was working in the kitchen.

What you learn from experiences like this is to stay calm, which is the key to everything, breathing slowly and thinking clearly. Getting stressed isn't going to help the situation; just keep the head.

Incidentally, that waitress who helped me became my partner and we're still together back in Glasgow after ten years!

Margo has an open kitchen which I really enjoy because it allows you to get a lot more feedback from the customers. For instance, they can see the guys and girls having fun in the kitchen which helps to make a happy atmosphere which is always a compliment to whoever's the leader in the kitchen.

I love working in Glasgow. Having worked away from the city for some time there's something about the people that draws you back. The people you work with can have a laugh and enjoy themselves, but they get on with it; the work ethic of Glaswegian people is excellent. That means as a head chef you can enjoy your work too as you've got people around you who want to get involved and that makes for a happy team and makes your job easier.

They say people make Glasgow, but laughter also makes the city; it's such an important quality to have, especially in hospitality.

"It's not about the person cooking, it's all about the food."

Sobrasada and guindilla croquettes, confit garlic emulsion

Ingredients

Cooked ham hough

Ham hough - 1

Onion - 1. Cut into large chunks for stock

Carrot - 1. Cut into large chunks for stock

Bay leaf - 1

Black peppercorns - 2

Croquette mix

Sobrasada - 40g

Plain flour - 28g

Whole milk - 100g

Pickled guindilla chillies - 8g. Finely chopped

Guindilla pickle liquor - 28g

Manchego - 20g. Grated on a micro-plane or fine grater

Picked ham hough - 35g

Flat parsley leaf - 5g. Chopped

Gelatine - 1/4 of a leaf. Soaked in cold water

Confit garlic emulsion

Neutral olive oil - 160g

Garlic cloves - 20g. Peeled

Egg white - 40g

Greek yogurt - 40g

Table salt - 10g

Croquette breadcrumbs

Flour - 40g

Sweet smoked paprika - 8g

Eggs - 2. Beaten

Panko breadcrumbs - 60g

To assemble

Manchego cheese - 30g

Pickled guindilla chillies - 10g. Finely sliced

Method

Serves 4

The ham hough Cover the ham hough in cold water in a large pan and bring to a boil. Skim any impurities that form on top, then add the rest of the ingredients. Reduce the heat to a very gentle simmer and poach for 3 – 4 hours or until tender. Remove from the heat and allow to cool slightly in the stock. Lift the ham hough out and pick off all the meat while it's still a bit warm. You'll be left with ham stock and some extra picked meat which you could use for a soup or stew.

The croquette mix In a pot, gently melt down the sobrasada over a medium heat, mix in the flour to form a roux and cook for 4 mins, stirring continuously. In a separate pot, bring the milk and pickle liquor to a simmer (it will look split, don't worry). Add the milk and pickle liquor into the sobrasada roux bit by bit, mixing each time until the liquid is fully incorporated. When all of the liquid has been added bring it up to a simmer to thicken.

Fold in the rest of the ingredients making sure the gelatine leaf has dissolved and everything is well incorporated. Transfer the mix to a suitable container and once cool enough, cover and chill in the fridge for a couple of hours or overnight.

Confit garlic emulsion Place the garlic cloves and oil in a small pan and confit on a low heat for 30 – 40 mins until the garlic is tender, then allow to cool to room temperature. Remove the garlic cloves, from the oil and add to a blender along with the salt, egg whites and yogurt, blend to a paste. On a medium speed, very slowly add the oil to the paste mixture in the blender to emulsify.

This recipe will make a bit more garlic emulsion than you need, but it can be used on our cod and black rice dish, or stored in the fridge for other uses.

The croquette breadcrumbs Once the croquette mix is chilled and firm you can shape into 30g balls. Set up three separate bowls or containers for coating the croquettes, one with flour, one with beaten egg and one with the paprika and panko breadcrumbs mixed together. Roll the balls in flour, dip in the egg and then the crumbs. Chill for at least an hour before deep frying.

To assemble Deep fry the chilled croquettes at 180°C until golden brown, this should take approximately 4 mins. Spoon small dots of garlic emulsion onto your plates for the croquettes to sit on, then spoon another small dot of emulsion on top of each croquette. Top each one with a pinch of sliced guindilla and finely grated manchego.

< Sobrasada and guindilla croquettes, confit garlic emulsion

Page 136 Lamb gigot, salsa verde, bonnet polenta

Cod, black rice, garlic cream, tempura sea vegetables

Ingredients

Confit garlic emulsion

Neutral olive oil - 160g

Garlic cloves - 20g. Peeled

Egg white - 40g

Greek yogurt - 40g

Table salt - 10g

Tempura sea vegetables

Samphire - 40g

Sea purslane - 40g

Cornflour - 80g. Plus and extra pinch for dusting

Glutenous rice flour - 50g

Table salt - 4g

Sparkling water - 250g. Ice cold. You can mix the ice cubes in with the batter

Squid ink rice

Garlic - 1 clove. Finely chopped

Carnaroli rice - 100g

Butter - 20g

Shallot - 100g. Finely diced

Squid ink - 5g

Tomato purée - 10g

Fish sauce - 5g

Chicken stock - 280g

White vermouth - 20g

To serve

Cod fillet - 4 x 100g – 150g portions. Skin removed

Neutral olive oil for frying

Table salt to season

Lemon - 1. Halved

Method

Serves 4

Confit garlic emulsion Place the garlic cloves and oil in a small pan and confit over a low heat for 30 – 40 mins until the garlic is tender, then allow to cool to room temperature.

Remove the garlic cloves, from the oil and add to a blender along with the salt, egg whites and yogurt, blend to a paste. At a medium speed, very slowly add the oil to the paste mixture in the blender to emulsify. This recipe will make a bit more garlic emulsion than you would normally need for this dish.

Tempura sea vegetables Combine the cornflour, rice flour, salt and iced sparkling water in a bowl, gently whisk to combine taking care not to over work the mixture. In a separate bowl dust the samphire and sea purslane in a pinch of cornflour in a bowl then knock off any excess. Dip the sea vegetables into the batter to coat, and fry at 180°C for 1 – 2 mins, or until crisp. Set aside on a piece of kitchen paper.

Squid ink rice In a wide pan, melt 15g of the butter and gently sweat the shallots. Add the rice and heat for a few mins, making sure not to brown the rice or shallots. Increase the heat and add half of the vermouth. Once the vermouth has reduced and all been absorbed stir in the tomato puree and squid ink.

In a separate pot, bring the stock to the boil. Start adding the stock to the rice one ladle at a time, allowing each ladleful to absorb before adding the next one. The rice and stock must both remain at a simmer at all times throughout cooking, keep stirring as you go. Once the stock has all been added, cook until the rice is just al dente and you have a loose risotto consistency. Add the remaining butter and vermouth and season with the fish sauce.

To serve Preheat a non-stick frying pan and lightly season the cod portions all over with table salt. Add the oil to the pan, followed by the cod portions. Cook until golden on one side then flip, and turn off the heat under the pan and allow to cook through the rest of the way in the residual heat, finish with a squeeze of lemon juice.

To plate, add the rice in a flattened pool at the bottom of each plate. Spoon a dollop of the garlic emulsion in the middle, and place the fish on top, followed by the crispy sea veg.

< Cod, black rice, garlic cream, tempura sea vegetables

Page 137 Lemon and sorrel posset

Lamb gigot, salsa verde, bonnet polenta

Ingredients

Braised gigot

Lamb gigot chops - 4
Large onion - 1. Sliced
Butter - 20g
Lamb stock - 1 litre
Rosemary - 4 sprigs
Red wine - 200g
Flour - 20g
Salt and pepper

Salsa verde

Mint leaves - 10g. Picked
Basil leaves - 10g. Picked
Flat parsley leaves - 30g. Picked
Egg yolk - 1
Dijon mustard - 10g
Cornichon - 10g
Lemon juice - 10g
Anchovy - 1
Extra virgin olive oil - 100g
Table salt - 1g

White polenta

White polenta - 100g
Bonnet (firm Scottish goats cheese) - 100g. Grated
Butter - 50g. Diced
Milk - 100g
Water - 500g
Salt - 5g

Method

Serves 4

Braised gigot Pre-heat an oven proof pot/casserole on the stove over a medium/high heat. Season the gigot chops in salt and pepper and sear on both sides until golden brown, you can do this in stages so as not to crowd the pan. Once the lamb has been seared and removed from the pan lower the heat. Gently fry the onions in the butter until soft, then add the flour. Bring the heat back up to high, add the red wine and reduce by half. Add the stock, rosemary and return the lamb.

Cover and braise in an oven at 160°C, for 3 – 4 hours or until fork tender but still holding their shape. Once cooked, remove the lamb from the pan and return the stock to the stove. Simmer to reduce it to a sticky gravy before returning the lamb to the pan.

Salsa Verde Blitz all of the ingredients together in a blender on high speed.

Polenta Bring the water and milk to a simmer, season with the salt. Whilst whisking, trickle in the polenta. Simmer and stir continuously for 10 mins. Turn off the heat and whisk in the butter and cheese immediately.

To assemble Spoon the polenta onto the plate and flatten slightly. Place the lamb on top and pour over some sauce, drizzle over some salsa verde.

Lemon and sorrel posset

Ingredients

Sorrel granita

Sorrel - 80g

Lemon - 2. Juice

Sugar - 40g

Water - 100g

Sorrel olive oil

Sorrel - 25g

Extra virgin olive oil - 25g

Sorrel and lemon curd

Eggs - 2

Lemon - 2. Zest and juice

Butter - 20g. Softened

Caster sugar - 20g

Sorrel leaves - 20g

A basin of iced water for cooling the mix

Method

Serves 4

Best to prepare this one the day before so that the posset has time to set, and the granita has time to freeze.

Sorrel granita In a jug blender blend water and sugar together until dissolved, then blend through the sorrel and lemon juice. Transfer to a container and freeze.

Sorrel olive oil Blitz together in a blender. Chill over ice to keep it vibrant green.

Sorrel and lemon curd Whisk eggs, sugar, lemon juice and zest in a mixing bowl to fully combine, then whisk in the softened butter. Place the mixing bowl over a pan of simmering water (bains marie) ensuring the base of the bowl isn't touching the water. Cook the curd mix over the bains marie, whisking continually until thickened (this will be at around 78°C). Once the curd mix has thickened, plunge the base of the bowl straight into the basin of ice water to prevent it from overcooking. Once chilled, transfer the curd mix and sorrel leaves into a blender and blitz until smooth. Divide between four serving glasses and chill in the fridge to set.

Lemon posset Bring the cream and sugar to a very gentle simmer. While that's heating, zest and juice the lemons into a separate bowl. Take the cream off the heat, add to the bowl with the lemon and quickly whisk. Allow to cool to room temperature. Once cooled, pour on top of the cooled curd in the glasses and set in the fridge.

Confit lemon zest Remove the zest from the lemon using a sharp knife or peeler, remove any white pith from the zest. Add the peels to a saucepan of cold water and bring to the boil. Remove the peel from the hot water, add to fresh cold water and bring to the boil again, repeating 3 times in total. Remove the peel from water a final time and once cool enough to touch, slice into thin strips. Return the strips to the emptied saucepan with the measured 25g of water and the caster sugar and heat until reduced by half.

To assemble Scrape the frozen granita with a fork, and spoon on top of the posset. Garnish with a few strips of the lemon zest and drizzle on the oil.

15

Barolo
Riccardo Venditti
Executive head chef
DRG Group

"Barolo is a reflection of Glasgow's dynamic food culture, combining traditional Italian/Scottish flavours with modern culinary techniques."

I first got involved in the restaurant trade in 2005 at the food academy in my native Italy. My father was an excellent cook, and I was always amazed by him and his food. His passion for cooking and wine inspired me to pursue a career in hospitality. My first job in Scotland was as a baker on the west coast and from there I worked with top chefs and learned to focus on quality ingredients, including buying direct from Italy.

Barolo reflects Glasgow's dynamic food culture, combining traditional Italian/Scottish flavours with modern culinary techniques. We focus on using locally sourced, exclusive Italian seasonal ingredients to create dishes that are both innovative and comforting. The atmosphere is warm and inviting, with a commitment to excellent service that makes every guest feel at home. Whether it's a casual meal or a special occasion, we strive to offer a dining experience that's memorable, with a menu that caters to a variety of tastes while highlighting the richness of Italian cuisine.

My 'food philosophy' is rooted in an open-minded approach to new techniques and a willingness to think outside the box. To me, dining is an experience that goes beyond just eating—it's about creating a connection through food, fostering community, and celebrating the joy that comes from sharing a well-crafted meal. I believe that everything starts with one core principle: quality + quality = quality. This means using the best ingredients and applying the highest standards on the detail in every aspect of cooking to deliver exceptional dishes. But also focusing on simplicity, have respect for the ingredients and not overcomplicating things.

One of the most challenging experiences in my culinary journey happened seven-to-eight years ago when I opened three restaurants. I faced serious issues with staff, and after an overnight meeting finished at 4am it seemed like everything was about to collapse. However, I woke up with a solution and managed to keep the restaurants open. The solution was to be refreshed and think outside the box.

The key lesson I learned from this experience is that no one is indispensable, including myself. It taught me the importance of adaptability and humility in leadership. I've come to understand that the strength of a team lies in its ability to work together and that everyone, no matter their role, can be replaced if necessary.

Glasgow is my current home. Managing a restaurant or being a head chef in Glasgow involves balancing creativity with the practical demands of the industry. The city is renowned for its vibrant food scene, so staying competitive means continuously innovating while maintaining consistency in quality which we strive to do constantly at Barolo.

My role in the DRG Group (not only Barolo) requires excellent leadership skills to manage a diverse team, often in a high-pressure environment, and strong organizational abilities to handle everything from sourcing ingredients and creating menus to controlling costs.

Additionally, understanding the local culture and customer preferences is crucial, as the city's culinary landscape is influenced by a mix of traditional Scottish/Italian cuisine and international flavours. Certainly, I feel at home in Glasgow and part of the community.

Frittatina carbonara

Ingredients

Béchamel sauce

Unsalted butter - 40g

Country Range plain flour - 40g

Whole milk - 500ml

Sea salt - A good pinch

Frittatina

Bucatini pasta - 60g

Egg yolk - 60g

Béchamel sauce - 125ml

Guanciale - 100g. Pan fried and cooled

Pecorino - 80g

Black pepper - A couple of turns

Batter

Water - 150ml

Strong Flour - 100g

Baking powder - 1/2 tsp

Breadcrumbs

Panko breadcrumbs - 200g

Pancetta coccante garnish

Pancetta - 250g. Sliced

Method

Serves 4

Pancetta garnish Start by making the pancetta garnish. Pre-heat the oven to 180°C. Place the pancetta on greaseproof paper on a baking tray and bake for 10 – 15 mins until crispy. Set aside to cool.

Bechamel sauce For the bechamel sauce, place a saucepan over medium heat and add the unsalted butter. Allow the butter to melt completely, swirling the pan occasionally to melt evenly and preventing the butter browning. Gradually add the flour to the melted butter, using a whisk to incorporate it smoothly. Stir constantly making sure all the butter is absorbed. It should start to become more paste-like. Keep stirring over a very low heat until it starts to smell nutty, or some say like toast. Slowly add the milk a little at a time, making sure it incorporates and loosens the paste before adding more. Keep adding a little at a time until you end up with a smooth consistency. Increase the heat to medium and bring the mixture to a gentle boil, stirring occasionally to prevent sticking. Once the sauce begins to bubble gently, reduce the heat to low to maintain a simmer. Simmer for 10 mins and then add in the salt and stir through.

Frittatina Boil the bucatini (broken into thirds) for 4 mins, then drain. Drizzle the cooked bucatini with extra virgin olive oil (to prevent sticking) and allow it to cool a little.

Place 125ml of the bechamel sauce in a bowl, stir in the guanciale, egg yolks, pecorino and the cooled pasta. Combine the ingredients well. Spread the mix out on a baking tray, cover with cling film and refrigerate for 30 mins.

Next, make the batter. Place the flour and baking powder in a bowl. Gradually add the water, whisking continuously until you have a smooth, lump free mix. Set aside.

Remove the frittatina mix from the fridge. The mixture will make 8 cakes. You can portion estimate or if you wish to weigh they will be around 100g each. Take each serving and form into round flat cakes.

Place the panko crumbs in a bowl and set beside your bowl of batter. Dip a cake in the batter, gently shaking off the excess. Next place in the panko crumbs and coat all over, pressing lightly to make sure the crumbs stick. Place on a tray and repeat with the other cakes.

Preheat your deep fryer to 170°C. Depending on the size of your fryer basket add 2 – 3 at a time and cook until golden brown in colour. Remove and drain the excess oil on kitchen paper. Serve with pancetta garnish.

< Frittatina carbonara

King prawn bisque

Ingredients

Whole king prawns - 500g
Butter - 40g
White onion - 70g
Garlic - 1 tbsp. Chopped
King prawn heads and shells
Cognac - 50ml
Tomato passata - 600g
Salt - To taste (add a little at first, adjust the seasoning at the end of preparation)

Method

Serves 4

Clean the king prawns, setting aside the heads and shells. Keep the cleaned king prawns aside and use the shells and heads for the initial phase of making the sauce.

In a saucepan, place the diced butter, onion, and garlic. Add the king prawn heads and shells, and begin cooking over low heat, stirring occasionally, until everything is golden brown.

At this point, deglaze with the cognac and let it evaporate.

Combine the tomato sauce and cook everything for about 50 mins, seasoning lightly with salt.

Once the sauce has cooked, strain it from the shrimp shells and heads using a spider or chinois, transferring them to a saucepan. Add no more than one liter of water to the shells and heads, bring to a boil to rinse the shells of their juices, then add the filtered water back into the finished sauce.

At this point, finely chop the shrimp tails with a knife.

Bring the sauce to a boil and add the chopped shrimp, cooking for another 15 mins approximately.

Let the sauce cool then place in a refrigerator.

Perle ai gamberoni

Ingredients

White onion - 80g
Double cream - 200ml
Extra virgin olive oil - 20ml
Sea salt - To taste
Chicche De Cecco (a type of pasta) - 800g
Cream of king prawns - 600g
King prawns meat cut in diced - 500g

Method

Serves 4

Begin by heating a drizzle of high-quality olive oil in a large saucepan over low heat. Allow the oil to warm gently without smoking.

Add finely diced onion to the warmed olive oil. Sauté the onion slowly over low heat, stirring occasionally to ensure even cooking. Cook until the onion becomes translucent and fragrant, but avoid browning.

Carefully pour the prepared king prawn bisque into the saucepan with the sautéed onion. The bisque should be smooth and rich, made from the shells and heads of the prawns, simmered to extract maximum flavor.

Increase the heat to medium-high to bring the bisque to a gentle boil. Stir occasionally to prevent sticking and ensure all ingredients are well incorporated.

Once the bisque is bubbling gently, pour in the cream. Use a spatula or wooden spoon to stir the mixture thoroughly. Bring it back to a boil, allowing the cream to meld with the bisque, creating a luxurious and velvety texture.

Taste the bisque and adjust seasoning as needed. Add a pinch of salt if necessary, ensuring the flavors are balanced and harmonious.

Carefully add diced king prawns to the simmering bisque. Stir gently to coat the prawns in the creamy sauce. Allow the prawns to cook in the bisque for approximately 2 mins, ensuring they are just cooked through and tender.

While the prawns are cooking, bring a separate pot of salted water to a rolling boil. Add Chicche De Cecco pasta to the boiling water and cook for exactly 2 mins. The pasta should be al dente – firm to the bite.

Drain the Chicche De Cecco pasta thoroughly, ensuring no excess water remains. Add the hot, cooked pasta directly to the simmering bisque and prawns. Stir gently to coat the pasta evenly with the creamy bisque sauce.

Continue cooking the pasta in the bisque sauce for an additional 30 secs – 1 min. This allows the pasta to absorb the flavors of the sauce and become perfectly coated and glazed.

Once the Chicche De Cecco pasta is well coated and glazed with the bisque sauce, remove the saucepan from heat. Serve immediately in warmed bowls, ensuring each portion is garnished with a sprinkle of fresh herbs or a drizzle of extra virgin olive oil for added flavor and presentation.

Finish by adding a drizzle of extra virgin olive oil and mix well. Serve the Chicche topped with freshly chopped parsley.

Smoked chicken parmigiana

Ingredients

Aubergines - 500g
Salt - For seasoning
Black pepper - For seasoning
Plain flour - As needed
Eggs - 3. Beaten
Chicken breast - 500g. Thinly cut
Extra virgin olive oil - 10g
Tomato passata - 600g
Fresh basil leafs - 20
Grated Parmesan cheese - 150g
Smoked provola cheese - 250g

Method

Serves 4

Aubergines Begin by heating a drizzle of high-quality olive oil in a large saucepan. With a potato peeler, peel the aubergines from the top to the bottom.

Cut the aubergines into 1.5cm thick slices. In a gastronom place the aubergine slices and season with salt on both sides.

In a gastronom, place the aubergine slices and flour them equally on both sides. Work the flour in with your hands. Let the aubergine layers stand for at least 5 mins. Remove the excess flour from the aubergine, either with your hands or with a sieve.

Quickly dip each aubergine in the eggs. Then fry 2/3 aubergine slices at a time at a temperature of 180°C for about 3 mins. Drain the aubergine slices on a paper towel and season with a pinch of salt on both sides. This must be done straight away when they're still hot. Cover the aubergines with some kitchen paper, and repeat the procedure with the next batches.

Chicken breast Cut the chicken breast into 4 thin slices, Season the chicken and quickley dip each chicken slice in the eggs then fry at a temperature of 180°C for about 3 – 4mins.

The parmigiana Sprinkle an even layer of extra virgin olive oil on the bottom of a tray, then add 300g of tomato sauce. Begin assembling the parmigiana.

First, place a layer of fried aubergine slices, overlapping each other – this is important.

Add 10 basil leaves and sprinkle 75g of Parmesan.

Add a layer of fried chicken.

Next, sprinkle the smoked provola on top.

Cover evenly with 300g of cold tomato sauce, spreading it from the sides toward the centre.

Repeat with another layer of fried aubergine slices (overlapping each other), 10 basil leaves, 75g of Parmesan, and fried chicken. Again, sprinkle the smoked provola on top.

Finish with a final layer of fried aubergine slices.

Cover evenly with 400g of cold tomato sauce, spreading from the sides to the center, and finish with a topping of Parmesan.

Preheat oven to 160°C and bake for 40 mins, covered with tin foil. Let it rest for 15 mins and serve.

Page 142/143 Perle ai gamberoni (with king prawn bisque)

< Smoked chicken parmigiana

> Birramisù

Birramisù

Ingredients

Zabaglione cream

Dark beer - 60 ml
Caster sugar - 130 g
Egg yolks - 150 g

Tiramisù cream

Double cream - 250ml
Mascarpone - 100g

The soaking syrup

Dark beer - 300ml
Strong espresso coffee - 200ml
Caster sugar - 20g

Birramisù cream base

Cold coffee and beer soaking syrup
Malt biscuits - 12 – 14
Dark coco powder - Dusting

Method

Serves 4

Zabaglione cream Whisk the egg yolks and sugar over a bain-marie using an electric whisk. After about 10 mins, when the mixture becomes frothy, gradually add the beer in a thin stream while continuing to whisk for another 10 mins (Note: ensure the beer is at room temperature). Once the mixture reaches a fluffy and foamy consistency, refrigerate immediately.

Tiramisù cream Whip the cream with the mascarpone until the mixture is well aerated and compact. Gradually add the zabaglione cream while continuing to whip for 10 – 15 mins, until the mixture is well aerated and has a consistent texture.

The soaking syrup Combine the sugar with the beer in a saucepan and bring to a boil, allowing the alcohol to evaporate. Then add the espresso coffee and let it simmer until slightly reduced. The soaking syrup should always be cold before using it.

Birramisù cream base Once ready, take the malt biscuits and begin to dip them in the coffee, soaking them for no more than 10 secs. Take serving glasses and start assembling the Birramisù by alternating layers in the following manner:

- Bottom layer of Birramisù cream
- Dusting of cocoa
- Soaked malt biscuit, 1
- Birramisù cream
- Dusting of cocoa
- Soaked malt biscuit, 1
- Birramisù cream

Leave a 2cm gap from the top and clean the edges of the glasses. Then, cover the tiramisù with wax paper and refrigerate them.

Before serving, sprinkle the surface with dark cocoa.

16 Partick Duck Club

Ross McDonald
Owner

I never had any grand plans of pursuing a career in hospitality. At sixteen and still at school, I landed a part time job at Cameron House on Loch Lomond, initially washing dishes, making tea and coffee and delivering room service. I spent a further two and a half years there working my way through the various departments, including the brasserie and fine dining restaurants, gaining great experience in a five-star resort.

While still working at Cameron House I enrolled in a Hospitality Management course at Glasgow Food Tech where I lasted a year. The excitement and buzz of working hands on in bars and restaurants outshone the academic side for me. From there I worked in several Glasgow restaurants and Hotels such as Brian Maule at Chardon D'Or, One Devonshire Gardens and Gordon Yuill & Co, where I met the person who would eventually become my business partner at the Duck Club, Greig Hutcheson.

When the time came to go out on our own, we had the frustration of bidding and losing out on several units in Glasgow before finally getting our hands on what had been the Rio Cafe, in Partick in Glasgow's West End which is where the Duck Club is today.

The name derives from some local history – there was a Duck Club of Partick over 200 years ago where merchants, bankers, professors and doctors would visit each Saturday and feast on duck, sage and onion from the river Kelvin, along with local ale. Having a bit of history as part of the name was important for us and ties in well with what we do; even one of our more senior guests remembers his grandfather telling him about the original club!

Partick Duck Club serves all day comfort food done well. We serve a wide variety of dishes and we're open all day for breakfast, brunch, lunch and dinner. Our restaurant is not too formal for a breakfast crowd, but, equally, not too relaxed for those wanting dinner. We cater for all demographics and have built up a fantastic, loyal following.

We make all our food here (except for our bread which we get from a local supplier) and all our staff work a four-day week which is vital to ensure everyone can have a life outside of work too.

Glasgow as a city doesn't have the sheer volume of population like London, or the tourist & festival attraction of Edinburgh so you need to work hard to get every single person through the door which means you must be on the ball all the time. Our loyal, regular customers consistently support us and have a sense of shared ownership with us which is vital for a restaurant in this city. They keep us on our toes. Added to that, we' re seeing more tourists coming into the city.

Since we opened in 2017, Partick has changed in a big way; there are so many restaurants & bakeries on our street alone. We got off to a slow start but following some great reviews, an AA rosette award and some extremely loyal customers we are busy most days now. Both our menus are available all day long and you can eat off them at any time – even if you want a duck leg and duck fat fry at 9am straight off the nightshift or a breakfast at 5pm straight out of your bed!

"We serve all day comfort food done well."

Pictured – Head Chef Jay Ward

Crispy Asian cauliflower

Ingredients

Head of cauliflower - 1

Soy glaze

Self raising flour - 1 cup
Cornflour - 1 cup
Cold water - 420ml
Rice wine vinegar - 1 tbsp
Salt - Pinch
Honey - 250ml
Rice wine vinegar - 50ml
Garlic - 2 cloves. Crushed
Red chillies - 2
Fresh ginger - 100g
Coriander seeds - 1 tsp

Batter

Self raising flour - 1 cup
Cornflour - 1 cup
Cold water - 420ml
Rice wine vinegar - 1 tbsp
Salt - Pinch

To finish

Coriander - Roughly chopped
Toasted sesame seeds
Red chillies - Sliced

Method

Serves 4

Soy glaze Place all ingredients in a deep pan and bring to the boil. Then set aside till cooled. Pass through a fine sieve, being left with a lovely sweet aromatic sauce.

Cut cauliflower into small bite sized florettes, set aside.

Batter Put water and rice vinegar in a large bowl, add salt and both flours and mix well. Should have the consistency of double cream.

In a large deep sauce pan add 4cm of vegetable oil and heat to 170°C.

Coat florettes fully in batter and fry until golden, best to do in 2 – 3 batches to avoid any clumping together.

To finish Drain on kitchen paper then coat in glaze and garnish with coriander, sesame and chilli.

< Crispy Asian cauliflower

Page 154 Roast duck leg, greens, creamed cauliflower and peppercorn sauce

Twice baked Orkney crab and black bomber souffle

Ingredients

Crab mix

Orkney white crab meat - 80g
Coriander - 30g. Chopped
Chilli flakes - 1 tsp
Lime - 1. Zested
Salt - Pinch

Souffle mix

Whole milk - 275ml
Butter - 40g
Plain flour - 40g
Black bomber cheese - 140g
Egg yolks - 50g
Egg whites - 100g
Mustard powder - Pinch
Cayenne pepper - Pinch
Nutmeg - Pinch
Salt - Pinch

Handful panko breadcrumbs & soft butter for greasing moulds.

Cheese custard mix

Double cream - 240ml
Parmesan - 30g
Egg yolk - 1
Salt - Pinch

Method

Serves 4

For the crab Combine all ingredients for crab mix and set aside in fridge.

For the souffle Melt the butter slowly in a heavy bottomed sauce pan, once melted add flour and spices and cook out for 4 – 5 mins. Slowly add the milk until combined with no lumps and is smooth and glossy.

Add the yolks and combine ensuring the mix does not boil. Take off the heat, add in the cheese and allow to cool. While cooling, whisk the whites to soft peaks and fold into the cooled mixture.

For the cheese custard mix Combine all the custard ingredients and mix well, then stir in the prepared crab.

Thoroughly grease 4 ramekins with the butter and then coat in breadcrumbs.

Fill each of the moulds with the souffle mix and place in a deep oven proof tray with roughly 2cm water in the bottom and bake for 12 – 15 mins. They should be slightly golden on top.

To serve Once cooled, remove carefully from moulds and place in individual (ideally cast iron) dishes for the second bake. Spoon over the crab and cheese custard mix and bake for 8 – 10 mins at 180°C.

Serve immediately.

< Twice baked Orkney crab and black bomber souffle

Page 155 Chocolate frangipane

Roast duck leg, greens, creamed cauliflower and peppercorn sauce

Ingredients

Duck legs - 4
Onion - 1
Garlic bulb - 1
Rosemary - 4 sprigs
Thyme - 1 bunch
Sugar - Pinch
Sea salt - 1 dessert spoon
Water - 1/2 cup

Greens - 500g. We use British tenderstem
Butter - 25g. Diced
Garlic clove - 1. Crushed

Cauliflower cream

Cauliflower - Small head
Double cream - 200ml
Whole milk - 100ml
Truffle oil - 1 tsp
Sea salt - Pinch
White pepper - Pinch

Peppercorn sauce

Green peppercorns - 125g
Beef jus - 500ml. Good quality
Double cream - 150ml
Shallot - 1. Diced
Rosemary - 1 sprig
Thyme - 1 sprig
Brandy - 25ml
Garlic - 2 cloves

Method

Serves 4

Prick the skins of the duck legs several times with a fork and season with the sea salt. Leave for 10 – 20 mins to draw moisture from the skin.

Chop cauliflower into small florettes, add to a pan with milk and cream and simmer until soft. Blend to a smooth consistency with a hand blender, season and finish with the truffle oil and set aside.

In a large frying pan sear the duck legs until the skins are golden, add onions and garlic and fry for 2 mins before transferring to an oven tray, then add the water, rosemary & thyme. Cover with foil and bake for 90 mins at 170°C. Remove from oven and allow to rest (still covered) for 30 mins.

For the sauce reduce beef jus in a pan by 1/3 and add peppercorns. Sweat off onions, garlic and herbs. Add brandy and burn off all the alcohol. Add double cream and bring to the boil. Remove from heat and allow to infuse. Add cream and check seasoning.

Lightly fry greens of choice in the butter and garlic.

To serve Build on plate with a large circle of cauliflower purée on the bottom, then the greens, sit the duck leg on top and finally pour over the peppercorn sauce.

Chocolate frangipane

Ingredients

Unsalted butter - 150g. Soft
Caster sugar - 150g
Whole eggs - 150g
Ground almonds - 150g
Plain flour - 30g
Vanilla pod - 1. Split and deseeded
54% chocolate drops - 100g
Flaked almonds - Handful

Method

In a mixer beat the sugar and butter until pale and almost double in size. Slowly add the eggs until all are well incorporated. Then add the vanilla seeds and mix well.

In a separate bowl, mix the ground almonds and the flour together and fold into the butter mix, along with the chocolate drops. Grease 4 x 10cm tart tins and divide mixture into each, and scatter the flaked almonds on top. Bake in oven for 8 – 10 mins at 180°C.

To serve Once cooled turn out onto plates. We like to serve with a spoon of Katy Rodgers crème fraiche and a drizzle of honey.

17 Ardnamurchan
Ryan Hawes
Head chef

"The freshest but also the best sourced Scottish food"

I was born in West Africa and my family moved back to Britain when I was young. At thirteen my dad announced that I was too old for pocket money, so I started doing washing up in a transport café. I loved it and developed a desire to become a chef. After a couple of stints in various diners, I wrote a spec letter to the Dorchester Hotel in London and landed a job as a chef there. Later, after ten years as head chef of three restaurants in London, I moved to Brazil with my wife and opened a food truck in Sao Paulo, before coming back to the UK for my daughter's education and working now in Glasgow, after a stint in Edinburgh, as head chef at Ardnamurchan.

If you're looking not only for the freshest but also the best sourced Scottish food, then Ardnamurchan is the restaurant for you. We have twenty suppliers, including five fishmongers and we source items from specific suppliers. We bring together simple ingredients, to make good, tasteful food. If it tastes good, make it simple.

I firmly believe that if an ingredient doesn't bring anything to the plate it shouldn't be there. I'll look at a food item including the colour, try to build up the fat, the acid, the spice or the puree until I'm happy with it. Colour shouldn't be everything on a dish. It is essential that you have confidence in what you're cooking.

It's also imperative you promote a happy atmosphere in the kitchen – they're too many knives there for a start! – because that translates quickly out to front of house and the customers. Working in a busy kitchen is high pressured, but as head chef you need to keep your cool. I often compare the role of the chef to a picture of a swan gliding gracefully on the surface of a pond. What you don't see is the swan's flapping legs below the water because the head chef keeps calm with a straight face. In the kitchen, there's a deadline every three minutes and that's the way it is.

In some kitchens it's regarded as heresy if the customer wants to change something at the last minute. For me that's no big deal. It's the customer's choice that keeps everything going and I make sure all the kitchen staff take that attitude.

There have been many changes in our trade. It's becoming more difficult to recruit and a lot of training opportunities for people coming into our profession have gone. There's also, rightly, a much greater focus on diets and allergies than before. But that keeps you focused on the customer's needs, and most importantly, their safety.

I love working in Glasgow, the people are great. They're approachable and give you good, constructive feedback. Scotland has some of the best ingredients and produce in the world. Scottish venison for example, is the best of its' kind anywhere. A simple, but delicious dish and as with everything else we do, we make sure that we prepare, cook and serve it at its best at Ardnamurchan.

Hebridean blue cheese, pear, smoked almonds, pickled shallots, dressed salad leaves, chives

Ingredients

Hebridrean blue cheese - 30g. Crumbled

Fresh ripe pear - 1. Cut into wedges

Smoked almonds - 20g. Roughly chopped

Red wine vinegar - 100ml

Water - 100ml

Salt - 1 tbsp

Sugar - 2 tbsp

Banana shallot - 1. Cut into rings

Finely chopped chives - 10g

Selection of the seasons salad leaves - 50g

Rapeseed oil - 3/4 cup

Red wine vinegar - 1/4 cup

Salt - 1 tsp

Cracked black pepper - 1/2 tsp

Maldon sea salt - 1/2 tsp

Method

First to pickle the shallots, place 100ml of red wine vinegar and water into a bowl, add the salt and sugar and whisk to dissolve, once dissolved add the shallot rings and leave for at least 2 hours to pickle before using.

To make the oil and vinegar dressing, place the rapeseed oil, vinegar, salt and pepper in a clean jar with a lid and shake to emulsify.

Place the salad leaves in a bowl with a little of the oil and vinegar dressing, adding a pinch of maldon salt to season the leaves.

To assemble the plate start with the wedges of fresh pear, then add the blue cheese and shallots, carefully arrange the salad leaves in and around the pear and cheese finally adding the smoked almonds and chives.

< Hebridean blue cheese, pear, smoked almonds, pickled shallots, dressed salad leaves, chives

Page 162 Venison pave, crispy potato terrine, pickled brambles, buttered cavolo nero, red wine...

Arnold Bennett omelette

Ingredients

Milk - 400ml

Smoked haddock - 100g

Butter - 20g

Plain flour - 20g

Large free range eggs - 2. Whisked together

Kintyre cheddar cheese - 100g

Finely chopped chives - 10g

Selection of the seasons salad leaves - 25g

Rapeseed oil - 3/4 cup

Red wine vinegar - 1/4 cup

Salt - 1 tsp

Cracked black pepper - 1/2 tsp

Maldon sea salt - 1 pinch

Method

Serves 1

To start the omelette place the milk in a pot and bring to gentle simmer, when warm add the smoked haddock and cook for around 3 mins or until the haddock starts to flake, then take the pot off the heat and leave to cool. Once the milk has cooled and been flavoured by the haddock drain the fish from the milk and weigh out 200ml of haddock milk. Melt the butter in a small pot and add in the flour whisk together then add in the milk, gently warm the white sauce whisking at the same time, when you have a smooth sauce add the cheese and whisk together until the cheese has melted.

Flake the cooked haddock and set aside until needed.

Now to make the omelette, add a little oil and 1 tbsp of butter to an omelette pan and heat gently, once the butter starts to foam add the beaten eggs and stir with a spatula until cooked. Once the eggs are cooked place the flaked haddock on top and then spoon over the white cheese sauce, then either place under a grill or finish with a blow torch to caramelize the top of the omelette.

To make the oil and vinegar dressing, place the rapeseed oil, vinegar, salt and pepper in a clean jar with a lid and shake to emulsify.

Place the salad leaves into a bowl with a little of the oil and vinegar dressing, adding a pinch of Maldon salt to season the leaves.

To assemble the plate simply arrange the dressed leaves on top of the omelette, sprinkle over the chopped chives and serve with warm buttered toast.

< Arnold Bennett omelette

Page 163 Caramelized lemon tart, raspberry coulis, raspberry sauce, fresh berries

Venison pave, crispy potato terrine, pickled brambles, buttered cavolo nero, red wine and bramble jus

Ingredients

Venison - 4 x 200g. Pave steak
Medium potatoes - 6 Maris piper
Butter - 250g block
Red wine - 175ml
Port - 175ml
Beef stock - 800ml
Shallots - 2. Finely chopped
Rosemary - 1 sprig
Butter - 6 tbsp
Fresh brambles - 100g
Fresh brambles for the pickled garnish - 16
Cavolo nero - 8 leaves. Center spine removed
Water - 100ml
Red wine vinegar - 100 ml
Maldon sea salt - 1 pinch
Salt - 1 tbsp
Sugar - 2 tbsp

Method

First to make the potato terrine, peel and thinly slice all the potatoes, wash the starch off and place in a bowl, melt the block of butter and add to the potatoes with some salt. Grease a terrine mould and line with baking paper, now start layering the potato in the terrine and continue until it is full. Cook the terrine at 180°C for 1 hour or until a knife easily goes through the potato, once cooked place a weight on top of the terrine and chill overnight, the next day turn out the terrine and slice one piece and put aside for later.

Next to make the red wine and bramble jus, place a cooking pot onto a medium flame and gently sauté the chopped shallots and rosemary sprig in cooking oil and 2 tbsp of butter, when cooked add both the red wine and port. Turn the flame up to a high heat and reduce by half. Once reduced add the beef stock and again reduce by half, then turn the heat down to a gentle simmer and add 100g of fresh brambles, continue to cook for a further 15 mins or until the fruit has broken down into the sauce. Pass the sauce through a fine sieve pushing all the fruit through, measure out 250ml and place in a small sauce pan on a low heat, once the sauce is warm whisk in 2 tbsp of butter and keep warm, being careful not to boil the sauce.

Now to pickle the brambles, take the red wine vinegar, water, sugar and salt and place in bowl, whisk together to dissolve both the sugar and salt, then add the brambles, leave to pickle for at least 2 hours before using.

Next to cook the Venison, pre heat the oven to 180°C and then place a heavy based frying pan on a high heat and add 2 tbsp of cooking oil, season the venison with salt and pepper and sear the outside all over in the frying pan, once you have achieved a nice even colour, turn the heat down and add 2 tbsp of butter, then baste the venison in the frying pan with the foaming butter for 2 mins, after this take the venison out of the pan and put on a roasting tray and place in the oven then cook to an internal temperature of 60°C, once this has been achieved leave the venison to rest for 5 mins before carving.

In order to bring the plate together warm 300ml of water in a small pot with 2 tbsp of butter, once the water/butter is hot blanche the cavolo nero leaves for 30 secs, then take out and season. Next warm a frying pan and add cooking oil and 1 tbsp of butter, when hot place the potato terrine in the frying pan and colour on both sides, once coloured take out of the pan and season with salt.

Now to plate up the dish top and tail the venison pave and stand up right on the plate sprinkle a little Maldon salt on the venison, then place the potato terrine next to the venison with a spoon of the jus in between, arrange the cavolo nero leaves on top and garnish with the pickled brambles.

Caramelized lemon tart, raspberry coulis, raspberry sauce, fresh berries

Ingredients

For the pastry case (optional)

Plain flour - 500g
Icing sugar - 140g
Unsalted soft butter - 250g
Egg yolks - 4
Or use a pre cooked tart base

For the filling

Eggs - 5
Caster sugar - 140g
Double cream - 150ml
Fresh lemons - 3. Juice and zest
Icing sugar
Fresh seasonal berries

Raspberry sauce

Fresh raspberries - 200g
Lemon juice - 20ml
Caster sugar - 3 tbsp
Raspberry sorbet - 4 balls. Good quality

Method

To make the pastry (if using) Mix the sieved flour, icing sugar together in a bowl, rub in the soft butter until you get a fine bread crumb texture, then add in the egg yolks and combine to make a dough, add a little water if the dough is too dry, flatten out the pastry with your hands until the thickness of a 1 pound coin, cover with cling film and chill for at least 30 mins in the fridge.

To make the filling place all the ingredients into a bowl and whisk together, check the taste and add either more sugar or lemon juice as needed.

Remove the pastry from the fridge and place in a 23cm tart tin making sure to press down into the edges, then place baking paper on top of the pastry and fill with dried beans. Blind bake the tart case in a pre heated oven at 140°C for 10 mins, then remove the baking paper and bake for a further 20 mins. Once the pastry is cooked fill with the lemon mixture and cook for 30 – 35 mins until the tart is just set, but still with a little wobble.

To make the fresh raspberry sauce Place the fresh raspberries, lemon juice and caster sugar in a blender and blend until smooth. Then pass through a fine sieve and store in the fridge ready for plating.

To finish the plate Cut a wedge from the lemon tart and dust with icing sugar, caramelize this with a blow torch and place on a plate along with some of the fresh raspberry coulis, some seasonal berries and a scoop of raspberry sorbet.

18

Ka Pao
Sandy Browning
Head chef

I started in hospitality when I left school at 18 and was looking for a summer job in between school and university. My older brother was a chef and he got me into a restaurant where I was expecting to be doing front of house but was introduced to the kitchen and spent most of my time there. Later that year I went onto university to study economics but after a while I decided that the kitchens were more for me. I loved the team aspect of working closely with others in the kitchen and being on my feet, active and always doing things rather than being stuck in an office.

Ka Pao is Southeast Asian inspired. I've worked in Bangkok for a while and used the techniques I learned there to marry a Scottish larder with South-East Asian influences while using as much home produce as possible. We obviously need to import some produce such as coconut and lemongrass, but we've got some of the best seafood and meat in the world here in Scotland. Unlike Southeast Asia with its warm wet climate, our climate is wet and cold, so our seasonal produce is very different but it's a lot of fun finding alternatives, like using rhubarb and gooseberry in salads instead of imported green mango.

At Ka Pao we want to deliver great food in an accessible way where anyone is welcome. We strive to have the menu well balanced so someone who loves spices can sit alongside someone who perhaps struggles with spices but can have a choice of something different. It's a restaurant where you can happily take generations of your family as a place for all occasions, where you can feel special but with no airs and graces. I think we've achieved that at Ka Pao as we've got all ages and cultures coming in. The team I'm working with are so multicultural which is one of the great things about Glasgow.

Ka Pao was my first head chef job and was one of my hardest challenges as we opened in January 2020 in Glasgow's West End and eight weeks later, we were shut due to Covid. The first two years were only intermittent, going from full service to serving only take aways with no music and the rules changing all the time. You realise when you're in a senior position in a business you've got a lot of people dependent on you and you need to look after your team. That's a steep learning curve, but one which I enjoyed every minute of, although it was tough.

Ka Pao's kitchen is an open kitchen, so you get to see guests enjoying their food. You also get to interact with the guests a lot as they chat with you and have a bit of banter about their food and Glasgow's is just up for that as it's a city where people wear their heart on their sleeve. I've worked in restaurants all around the world and Glasgow is second to none when it comes to people enjoying their dining experience.

One of my favourite things about our trade is that one of our main aims is to make people happy. There are not many jobs where you get to do that. How often do you get people coming up to you and thanking you for the job you do but in dining that happens to us almost daily.

"Marrying a Scottish larder with Southeast Asian influences"

Grilled Duke of Berkshire pork neck, whisky jaew

Ingredients

Whisky jaew (dressing)

Caster sugar - 60g
Peeled garlic cloves - 30g
Lemongrass - 10g. Thinly sliced
Fresh lime juice - 100g
Soy sauce - 100g
Sweet soy sauce - 50g
Chilli powder - 2g
Talisker 10-year-old single malt - 20g

To assemble

Duke of Berkshire pork neck steaks - 4 x 150g
Whisky jaew to dress
Watercress or other peppery leaves - Bunch
Coriander leaves - Bunch
Fried sliced garlic - 5g
Fried chilli rings - 2g
Fried makrut lime leaf - 2g

You can deep fry your own lime leaves, garlic and chilli rings, or to make it easier you can find great crunchy toppings in an Asian supermarket to garnish

Method

Serves 4

Whisky jaew (dressing) Blend all of the ingredients together with a jug or stick blender until the garlic and lemongrass are fully incorporated. The dressing should be sweet, salty, and then smoky from the whisky. If Talisker isn't available, another peated whisky would still work well.

To assemble In the restaurant, we cook our pork neck overnight for 12 hours at 63°C. If you have a sous vide machine at home, great, if not then you could use pork loin, or any good steak would be perfect also. Something with a bit of fat will always work well. For service we cook our pork neck over coals, so this dish is a great one to do on the barbecue for the few days of sunshine we get in Glasgow. Season the steaks with table salt and then place them on the grill. Grill on both sides to achieve a lovely golden brown colour. Once the meat is warm in the middle take off to rest, then thinly slice. Place a carved steak on each plate, cover with the whisky jaew, garnish your herbs and leaves and sprinkle over fried garlic, chilli rings and lime leaf.

< Grilled Duke of Berkshire pork neck, whisky jaew

Page 170 Jungle curry of hand-dived scallops, pork belly and krachai

Arbroath smokie miang, galangal, spinach leaves and peanuts

Ingredients

Miang paste

Galangal - 10g. Finely chopped. Or ginger to substitute

Red bird's eye chilli - 1. Finely sliced

Shrimp paste - 5g

Brown shrimp - 10g

Toasted desiccated coconut - 30g

Caramel

Palm sugar - 200g

Water - 50g

Fish sauce - 60g

Concentrated tamarind paste - 45g

Miang paste - 1 tsp

To assemble

Arbroath smokie - 200g. Skin and bones removed and flaked

Miang caramel - 200g

Roasted and crushed peanuts - 120g

Toasted desiccated coconut - 60g

Diced ginger - 25g

Green bird's eye chillies - 8. Thinly sliced (can adjust amount to taste)

Shallot - 65g. Sliced

Granny smith apple - 100g. Diced

Lime - 35g. Diced. Skin still on

Spinach leaves to serve

Method

Serves 6 as a snack

Miang paste Combine all ingredients in a pestle and mortar and crush to a fine paste.

Caramel Combine sugar and water and heat until sugar has fully dissolved. Add fish sauce and allow it to come back up to a simmer. Add in the miang paste next and cook it out in the caramel for roughly 5 mins. Take off heat and mix in the tamarind. You'll have some miang caramel left over, but you can keep it in the fridge as a dressing or to make again.

To assemble Mix all ingredients together except the spinach leaves. Any smoked fish would work well with this dish if smokies aren't available. Chilli is a preference also so if you're not a huge fan of heat reduce the amount or add in bit by bit. It would go great with gem lettuce cups also. This dish should be sweet, spicy, nutty, bitter. It has a lot going on and is a great way to wake up your taste buds for the meal ahead.

< Arbroath smokie miang, galangal, spinach leaves and peanuts

Page 171 Bare Bones chocolate mousse

Jungle curry of hand-dived scallops, pork belly and krachai

Ingredients

Jungle curry paste

Red birdseye chillies - 30g

Maldon sea salt - 4g

Lemongrass - 25g. Fibrous outer layer removed and thinly sliced

Krachai (or ginger if unavailable) - 25g

Shallots - 25g. Peeled

Garlic cloves - 15g. Peeled

Shrimp paste - 4g

Coriander stems - 3g

To assemble

Scallops - 12. Large

Chicken stock - 400g. If not making your own buy a good quality fresh one

Jungle curry paste - batch

Pork belly - 200g. Cut into chunky lardons (thick streaky bacon would work well too)

Spring onion - 80g. Sliced

Krachai - 20g. Sliced

Makrut lime leaves - 8. Torn

Thai basil leaves - 20g. Picked

Fish sauce - To taste

Method

Serves 4

Jungle curry paste Blitz all ingredients together in a small food processor or pound in a pestle and mortar until you have a smooth paste. Add a touch of water if it's not coming together.

To assemble Heat up a wok and add a tablespoon of vegetable oil. Add in the pork belly or bacon and cook for a few mins until golden brown. Next, add in the jungle paste, spring onion and lime leaves and simmer for another two mins until it is fragrant. Add in the chicken stock and turn down the heat to a low simmer.

Next, pre-heat a separate pan to cook your scallops. Season them with table salt and then sear them in oil until they are golden brown on one side. Turn them over and cook for a further 1 – 2 mins. Remove from the pan and season with maldon sea salt.

Go back to the jungle curry sauce, season to taste with fish sauce and turn off the heat. At this point add the Thai basil and sliced krachai. The curry should be a spicy broth and go perfectly with the meaty, sweet scallops.

Arrange three seared scallops in each warm bowl and top with the jungle curry broth. Serve with a bowl of steamed jasmine rice on the side.

Bare Bones chocolate mousse

Ingredients

Chocolate mousse

Free-range egg yolks - 2. Large

Whole milk - 150g

Bare Bones Dominican 68% salted chocolate - 175g

Double cream - 180g

Sriracha honeycomb

Sugar - 110g

Glucose - 40g

Water - 20ml

Honey - 70g

Bicarbonate of soda - 16g

Sriracha - 12g

Method

Serves 4

Chocolate mousse Heat milk in pan to 85°C. Whisk the egg yolks in a mixing bowl while slowly adding the warm milk. Keep whisking so they don't scramble.

Return the milk and egg yolks to the pan and cook over a low heat. Keep stirring continuously and cook until the mixture coats the back of a spoon (roughly 2 mins).

Break up the chocolate into a mixing bowl and pour over the warm milk and eggs. Fold gently until it forms a ganache, then let cool till room temperature.

Whisk cream to soft peaks and then fold into the ganache mix. Divide into four 4 glasses and set in the fridge.

Sriracha honeycomb Make sure to use a pan which is large enough, a high walled 1.5l pan or bigger should be used as the caramel will quadruple in volume when you add the bicarbonate of soda, it will be very hot. Line a heatproof metal baking tray with butter and greaseproof paper before you start.

Put all ingredients apart from the sriracha and bicarbonate of soda into a pan and heat to 156°C, using a sugar thermometer to measure.

Remove from the heat and very carefully whisk in the sriracha. Return to the heat and bring back up to 152°C then remove again and carefully whisk in the bicarbonate of soda.

Immediately transfer the mixture to the lined metal tray and leave to cool. If you have any leftover honeycomb, it will keep perfectly in an airtight container in the freezer.

To serve When you're ready to serve break up chunky shards of the sriracha honeycomb and serve alongside the glasses of chocolate mousse.

19

Café Gandolfi
Seumas McKiness
Owner

Pictured with Seumas McKiness – Head Chefs, Alasdair McKiness and Jamie MacDonald

"We've retained the same staff for over forty years now and they know about the customers and take care of them."

I always wanted to work in hospitality. What motivated me further in this endeavour was an older couple who lived next door to my parents and took me to fancy restaurants which I loved. I was particularly impressed by the old St Enoch Hotel in Glasgow which was so grand and elegant. I wanted to be a part of this.

So, I studied Hotel Management and when I completed the course, I thought I would be able to go straight into managing and running a restaurant. Of course, like everybody else, I had to start in the kitchen at the bottom, in my case as a Kitchen Porter in Café Gandolfi back in 1983 where I've been ever since and which I'm now the owner of.

When I first became the owner, I wanted to both cook and manage at the same time, but customers were always wanting to see you and it became a strain trying to do both. So, I stayed at the front of house and employed excellent staff to look after the food and the kitchen. I'm delighted to say those staff have stayed with me ever since.

Despite its Italian sounding name – after a type of camera – Café Gandolfi is first and foremost a Scottish restaurant. We buy the best Scottish produce from local suppliers seasonally and treat it with respect. There are a number of core dishes which we tend to stick to, such as a great range of Stornoway black pudding – we were the first to serve this as a non-breakfast dish and put it on the map - because that's what people want. Led by our two fantastic head chefs, my son Alaisdair MacInnes and Jamie MacDonald, we prepare and serve them with a twist that keeps us fresh and which the customers love and attracts new custom.

Café Gandolfi is a one-off with its distinctive ambience and interior including stained glass designed by John Clark and unique furniture made by Tim Stead. It's located in a lovely setting right in the middle of the bustling Merchant City.

As I said we've mostly retained the same staff for many years, and they know about the customers and take care of them. We've got the children and grandchildren of customers coming back to us. At any one-time half of the people in the restaurant, which is always busy, will be regulars. But we're also attracting new customers, so we've got a good balance. We also place a great premium on maintaining great quality and standards; we never compromise on those.

What's the secret behind retaining high standards, customers and staff? That, essentially, comes down to teamwork. Nothing works in Café Gandolfi without the team and I'm part of that. Staff are our most important asset, and I encourage all our staff to buy into the product. In return we offer in-house training and flexibility which allows younger staff to fit in with their childcare and domestic arrangements.

We've had forty plus years of fantastic business and happiness with the restaurant despite recessions and a pandemic. I love Glasgow and the fact that Café Gandolfi has retained its status as a jewel at the heart of the Merchant City.

> Gandolfi Cullen Skink

Gandolfi Cullen Skink

Ingredients

Potatoes - 4 medium. Peeled and diced
Double cream - 300ml
Whole milk - 300ml
Water - 250ml
Smoked haddock - 300g
Butter - 60g
Onion - 1. Finely chopped
Olive oil - 1 tbsp
Mace or nutmeg - Pinch
Black pepper

A classic Gandolfi dish. We often have customers requesting the recipe – and luckily, it's in our cookbook. But for the real experience there's nothing like tucking yourself away in the corner of the Café and having a warm bowl of cullen skink brought to the table as you relax with friends.

Method

In a saucepan large enough to take all the ingredients, sauté the onions in butter and oil until soft.

Add the water to pan along with the potatoes and simmer for 5 mins.

Stir in the milk and cream and simmer for a further 5 – 10 mins until the potatoes are tender.

Cut the haddock into 2cm squares and drop into the soup. Continue to cook gently for 10 mins. Check seasoning and add the mace or nutmeg.

Black pudding and haddock Scotch egg, curried mayonnaise and charred pickled onion

Ingredients

Stornoway black pudding - 500g
Chopped smoked haddock - 300g
Eggs - 8
HP Sauce - 2 tbsp
Limes - 2
Panko breadcrumbs - 300g
Plain flour - 100g
Curry powder - 4 tsp
Ginger powder - 2 tsp
Cardamom powder - 1 tsp
Mayonnaise - 250g
White onion - 1
Water - 100g
White wine vinegar - 100g
Brown sugar - 100g

Method

Pickled onion Place the water, vinegar, sugar and onion in a small pot (so when you add the onion its fully submerged in the pickle liquor).

Bring to a simmer on a medium heat. Cook for 25 – 30 mins until soft.

Remove onion from the liquor and cut in half.

Heat up a pan until smoking.

Place a splash of oil and then the onion face down in the hot pan. Once charred remove and half again.

Curry mayonnaise In a pan combine all spices and toast until fragrant.

Mix the spice mix and the mayonnaise with the juice of one lime.

Scotch egg Bring a pot of water to a rolling boil. Place 4 eggs in the boiling water and boil for 6.5 mins (for a soft yolk).

Remove eggs and place immediately into iced water to stop the cooking.

Meanwhile bring your Stornoway black pudding to room temperature. Combine Black pudding, smoked haddock, hp sauce and the juice of the last lime together in a food processor and blitz until all has combined.

Split the mixture into four and roll into a ball then flatten. Place the egg in the centre of the mix and wrap the mixture evenly around the egg.

Next to bread the eggs place the flour, panko breadcrumbs and eggs in separate bowls. Beat the eggs.

Place each egg into flour first, then into the egg mixture. Next, coat with the breadcrumbs. Repeat the process – back into the egg, and back into the breadcrumbs for an extra crispy finish.

Deep fry for 7 mins at 170°C then finish in the oven for a further 4 mins.

To serve The scotch egg is served with the curry mayo placed down first in the centre of the plate in a small circle, the scotch egg is halved and placed on top of the mayo with the shallots on top.

< Black pudding and haddock Scotch egg, curried mayonnaise and charred pickled onion

Page 178 Pork and 'nduja ragu, potatoes 3-ways and pickled shallots

Pork and 'nduja ragu, potatoes 3-ways and pickled shallots

Ingredients

Sauce

Olive oil - 1 tbsp

Onions - 2

Carrot - 1

Celery - 3 sticks. Finely diced (mirepoix)

Garlic - 4 cloves

'Nduja - 100g

Fresh thyme - 1 tsp

Tomato puree - 2 tbsp

Pork mince - 500g

Nutmeg - 1 pinch

Chicken stock - 600ml

Tinned chopped tomatoes - 400g

Smoked mash

Floury potatoes - 1.5kg. Cut into equal sized chunks

Milk - 200ml

Butter - 100g

Smoked sea salt plus extra to serve.

Roast potatoes

Floury potatoes - 800g. Like maris pipers. Chopped into large even sized chunks

Vegetable oil - 60ml

Method

The sauce In a large pot (big enough to hold all the liquid) warm olive oil on a medium heat. Add the mirepoix vegetables with a little salt and soften for 10 mins.

Using a fine grater, mince the garlic cloves and stir into the pan along with the fresh thyme leaves. Cook 2 mins.

Add the 'nduja and tomato puree and mix into the mirepoix, cooking 3 mins.

Add the pork mince and turn up the heat slightly. Add a pinch of nutmeg and a further pinch of salt. Using a spoon, break the mince up into smaller pieces, turning constantly so the mince is coated in the 'nduja paste. Cook 5 mins.

Add the tin of chopped tomatoes and chicken stock and stir thoroughly.

Bring the pan to the boil, then lower the heat so the pan is gently bubbling. Pop a lid on the pan and cook for an hour.

Remove the lid, give everything a stir and cook 10 mins more with the lid off.

Take off the heat and check seasoning ready to serve.

Smoked mash Boil potatoes in a large pan of water for 20 – 25 mins until mashable. Drain well.

In the same saucepan (no need to clean it), bring the milk, butter and a few pinches of smoked salt to the boil. Take of the heat and mash the potatoes into the hot milk, beating until completely combined.

Roast potatoes Preheat the oven to 190°C fan. Fill a tray with 60ml vegetable oil (or duck fat if you have it) and put into the oven to heat up.

Boil the potatoes and their peelings for 8 – 10 mins in salted boiling water. Allow to steam dry 5 mins (remove the peelings), then gently rough up the edges and sprinkle with 1 tbsp of flour.

Coat the potatoes in the hot fat and cook for 45 mins – 1 hour, turning to ensure even, crisp cooking.

Shoestring fries

Maris Piper potatoes - 500g. Scrubbed

Vegetable oil - 1l

Salt and black pepper - Plenty

Pickled shallots

Banana shallots - 4

White wine - 100ml

White wine vinegar - 100ml

Water - 100ml

Caster sugar - 100g

Rock salt and pepper

Shoestring fries You will need either a mandolin or potato peeler with little teeth, since you are looking for julienne strips (like long matchsticks). Once you have a pile of strips, working in batches squeeze all the moisture out of the potatoes in a clean tea towel.

Place the oil in a large saucepan over a med-high heat. The level of oil should be no more than one quarter of the way up the pan. Test the oil is hot enough by dropping in a few strips of potato – when they bubble and turn golden after 20 secs the oil is hot enough.

Take a small handful of strips and untangle to loosen the strands – you want a batch that is not too packed together, so they form a messy bundle in the hot oil and are easier to flip over. Drop them carefully into the hot oil and cook for 90 secs until golden. Use tongs to flip the potatoes and do the same on the other side.

Once golden, remove with a slotted spoon and drain on kitchen paper. Repeat until all the fries are cooked. Wait a few mins between cooking batches as the oil needs to heat up.

Toss the fries in salt and pepper, ready to serve.

Pickled shallots Cut the shallots into 2mm thin slices and place in a large bowl.

Bring the wine vinegar, water and sugar to a simmer over a medium heat, stirring.

Simmer for 1 min, then pour the pickling liquor over the shallots. Season with salt and pepper.

Transfer to a clean container, seal and leave for at least 6 hours before serving.

Stored in a sterilised jar in the fridge these pickled shallots will keep for a month.

To assemble the dish Arrange the mash, then the roast potatoes, followed by the ragu. Top with shoestring fries and pickled shallots.

> Walnut tart

Walnut tart

Ingredients

Walnuts - 220g
Ritz biscuits - 32
Caster sugar - 350g
Egg whites - 6
Baking powder - 1 tsp
Vanilla extract - 1 tsp

My mother used to make this tart in the '70s – it's such a timeless recipe that it has become a classic in my home too. Simple yet rewarding – I urge you to give it a try, you might find it becomes a favourite for you as well.

Method

Pre-heat oven to 180°C. Line and grease a 23cm springform tin. Place the walnuts and biscuits into a food processor and blitz. Whip the egg whites until stiff and then slowly add the sugar continuing to beat.

Fold in the nut mixture and the vanilla and baking powder. Bake for 22 mins. Allow to cool before slicing.

20 Ho Wong
Tony Chung
Owner

I started out working in my father's Chinese takeaway in the Clyde seaside town of Saltcoats back in 1972. Later, I worked in a busy Chinese restaurant my father owned in Glasgow city centre called China Palace which gave me invaluable experience of operating and eventually managing and owning my own restaurant.

With my brother-in-law, David Wong, we opened the first Ho Wong in 1985. It quickly became very popular, including with celebrities and established itself as a Glasgow culinary landmark. Unfortunately, the site of the restaurant became subject to redevelopment and a compulsory purchase order. Regrettably, we had to close in 2019.

It was my intention to lead a quiet life and give up hospitality, but we came under a lot of pressure from our incredibly loyal, regular customers to reopen. So, I looked for a suitable venue and found a new building right in the middle of the busy commercial district in the city which we refurbished.

Unfortunately, Covid struck, but we were eventually able to open in December 2021. At first, we were concerned, after the length of time we'd closed that customers wouldn't come back. But, right from the moment we reopened, we've been incredibly busy, not least because our regular, loyal customers came back, and we've gained many more new ones.

At Ho Wong we strive for a unique blend of excellent fresh food sourced locally. Our menu hasn't changed since we first opened in 1985 because our customers love that menu; we offer what our customers want. Our focus is on serving the highest quality of beef, chicken and seafood (which is delivered fresh daily).

If you asked me to sum up what we do at Ho Wong I would say that we serve Chinese food tweaked and adapted for suitability to western palates.

Our new premises are more up-to-date and modern with a lovely ambience while retaining great service and a fantastic atmosphere. We've also got discreet rooms for events and private dining.

Over the years it's been immensely satisfying to watch the children and grandchildren of customers who came to us when we first opened, now become regular customers and bring their own children. We still have a flow of celebrities dining with us and were delighted to have Rick Stein give us a great write-up.

We've got a fabulous team at Ho Wong. They're all full-time, passionate and care for their customers and provide great service. The head chef, Eric, ensures the quality of the food is of the highest standard. It's a family run restaurant, and all the staff are part of the Ho Wong family.

We also encourage new ideas from the staff about the menu while retaining the basic formula which has worked so well for us and which our customers love.

Ho Wong provides something for everyone from all backgrounds and ages in a dynamic, buzzing atmosphere in the heart of the city. Why not come and try it.

"Providing something for everyone from all backgrounds and ages in a dynamic, buzzing atmosphere in the heart of the city."

Pictured – Head Chef Eric Fong

Crispy sea bass with sweet chilli sauce

Ingredients

Sea bass fillets - 2

Fresh Birds Eye chilli - 1/2 . Finely chopped

Diced onion - 1 – 2 tbsp. Diced

Diced pepper - 1 – 2 tbsp. Diced

Tomatoes - 2 – 3. Boil then blend into a puree with a pinch of salt

Sweet chilli sauce - 1 – 2 tbsp

Vegetable oil

Method

Serves 1

Place sea bass fillets on kitchen towel and ensure fish fillets are nice and dry.

Shallow fry the fillets in medium to high heat for 3 – 4 mins. Take the fish out and drain off excess oil.

Heat wok and throw in diced onions, peppers, tomato puree and fresh chili then add a tablespoon of sweet chilli sauce.

Season with salt then pour the sauce on the sea bass fillets. Serve with steamed rice.

Salt and chilli king prawns

Ingredients

Large king prawns - 8 – 10

Self raising flour - 200g

Water - 190g

Potato starch - 1 – 2 tbsp. Enough to coat the prawns

Diced onions - 1 – 2 tbsp. Diced

Diced peppers - 1 – 2 tbsp. Diced

Fresh Birds Eye chilli - 1/2. Finely chopped

Salt and pepper

Five spice - A pinch

Vegetable oil

Method

Serves 1

Place king prawns on kitchen towel to drain off any excess water.

Heat wok.

Dust king prawns with potato starch.

Add a little oil and ensure wok is smoking hot.

Throw king prawns in the wok then onions, peppers and fresh chilli. Cook for 2 – 3 mins then season with salt and a pinch of five spice.

Serve with soft noodles.

< Crispy sea bass with sweet chilli sauce

< Salt and chilli king prawns

Crystal king prawns

Ingredients

Large king prawns - 8 – 10

Self raising flour - 200g

Potato Starch - 1 – 2 tbsp. Enough to coat the prawns

Chopped spring onions - 1 – 2. Finely chopped

Cold water - 190g

Vegetable oil

Sweet and sour sauce - Optional

Method

Serves 1

Heat oil.

Place king prawns on kitchen towel to drain off any excess water. Mix the salt with self raising flour and add water to the flour until a thick consistency is formed.

Dust the king prawns with potato starch then dip into the batter mix and sprinkle with spring onions.

Place the king prawns into the hot oil and fry for 4 – 5 mins until golden brown.

Drain off any excess oil.

Serve with sweet and sour sauce.

Banana fritters

Ingredients

Banana - 1. Ripe

Self raising flour - 200g

Cold water - 190g

Golden syrup - 1 tbsp

Vanilla ice cream - 1 ball

Desiccated coconut - A sprinkling

Oil

Method

Serves 1

Slice banana in half.

Add water to the flour until a thick consistency is formed.

Drop the bananas into the batter mix then deep fry for 1 – 2 mins until golden brown.

Drain off excess oil.

Place on plate and drizzle a tablespoon of golden syrup on the bananas, scoop vanilla ice cream and sprinkle with desiccated coconut.

< Crystal king prawns

< Banana fritters

Restaurant details

Swadish
33 Ingram Street, Glasgow,
G1 1HA.
0141 553 0581
www.swadish.co.uk

Ox and Finch
920 Sauchiehall Street, Glasgow,
G3 7TF.
0141 339 8627
www.oxandfinch.com

Kelp
114 Cowcaddens Road, Glasgow,
G4 0HL.
0141 332 4032
www.kelp-restaurant.com

Brett
321 Great Western Road,
Glasgow, G4 9HR.
0141 406 0284
www.brettrestaurant.co.uk

Crabshakk
18 Vinicombe Street, Glasgow,
G12 8BG.
0141 286 4507
www.crabshakk.co.uk

Celentanos
28-32 Cathedral Square,
Glasgow, G4 0XA.
0141 552 3519
www.celentanosglasgow.com

The East End Fox
192 Glasgow Road, Glasgow.
G69 6EU.
0141 286 2598
www.theeastendfox.com

Eusebi Deli
152 Park Road, Glasgow,
G4 9HB.
0141 648 999
www.eusebideli.com

Partick Duck Club
27 Hyndland Street, Glasgow,
G11 5QF.
0141 334 9909
www.partickduckclub.co.uk

Crossbasket Castle Hotel
Stoneymeadow Road,
East Kilbride, G72 9UE.
01698829461
www.crossbasketcastle.com

Cail Bruich
725 Great Western Road,
Glasgow, G12 8QX.
0141 334 6265
www.cailbruich.co.uk

La Lanterna
35 Hope Street, Glasgow,
G2 6AE.
0141 221 9160
www.lalanterna-glasgow.co.uk

Barolo
92-94 Mitchell Square, Glasgow,
G1 3NQ.
0141 221 0971
www.barologrill.co.uk

Atlantic Brasserie
12 St Vincent Place, Glasgow,
G1 2DH.
0141 221 0220
www.atlanticbrasserie.co.uk

The Gannet
1155 Argyle Street, Glasgow,
G3 8TB.
0141 204 2081
www.thegannetgla.com

Margo
68 Miller Street, Glasgow,
G1 1DT.
0141 739 0882
www.margo.restaurant

Ardnamurchan
325 Hope Street, Glasgow,
G2 3PT.
0141 353 1500
www.ardnamurchan.biz

Ka Pao
26 Vinicombe Street, Glasgow,
G12 8BE.
0141 483 6990
www.ka-pao.com

Café Gandolfi
64 Albion Street, Glasgow,
G1 1NY.
0141 552 6813
www.cafegandolfi.com

Ho Wong
56 Waterloo Street, Glasgow,
G2 6HQ.
0141 221 3550
www.howongglasgow.com

Recipe index

Ferrier Richardson

Ferrier Richardson is one of Scotland's finest and best-known chefs. He has travelled the world extensively, representing Scotland for multi-national companies and government departments.

Earlier in his career he was responsible for re-establishing the culinary reputation of The Rogano and The Buttery, he was the opening Executive Chef for Glasgow's first Five Star Hotel and has owned several multi award winning restaurants that have featured in all the major guidebooks.

He is a Gold Medallist at The Culinary Olympics, Food Asia, Team manager of the award winning Scottish and British Culinary Olympic teams and was crowned Scotland's Master Chef of The Year.

Currently he owns the multi award winning Gastro Pub, The East End Fox based in the east end of Glasgow and the Auldhouse Arms in East Kilbride, that specialise in elevated comfort food.

Over and above this, he works privately worldwide and has a client list that includes Royalty, Presidents, A list celebrities, world class international sport stars and extremely high net worth individuals.

He prides himself on the quality of his food, professionalism and the privacy of his clients.

His food philosophy is to source the best ingredients and allow them to speak for themselves in his meticulously crafted dishes.

This is his eighth book in the On A Plate Series. Previous editions have included Glasgow, Edinburgh, Scotland, Manchester, Dublin and London.